P9-BAU-909

180 *more*

Random House Trade Paperbacks New York

180 *more*

EXTRAORDINARY POEMS FOR EVERY DAY

Selected and with an Introduction by

Billy Collins

A RANDOM HOUSE TRADE PAPERBACK ORIGINAL

Copyright © 2005 by Billy Collins

All rights reserved. Published in the United States by Random
House Trade Paperback, an imprint of The Random House
Publishing Group, a division of Random House, Inc., New York.

RANDOM HOUSE TRADE PAPERBACKS and colophon are
registered trademarks of Random House, Inc.

Owing to limitations of space, permission acknowledgments begin
on page 361.

CIP information is available upon request.

ISBN 0-8129-7296-1

Random House website address: www.atrandom.com

Printed in the United States of America

9 8 7 6 5 4 3 2

Text design by Barbara M. Bachman

contents

Billy Collins

POETRY, AMERICA'S LONGEST-RUNNING POETRY MAGAZINE, recently staged in its pages a debate between the poets Dana Gioia and August Kleinzahler. The subject on the table was an anthology called *Good Poems*, edited by Garrison Keillor. The opinions of the principals were so predictably extreme—Gioia thumbs up, Kleinzahler thumbs low down—the match could have been arranged by the World Wrestling Federation: Mister Necktie vs. The Shin-Kicker. At the risk of oversimplifying the exchange, I would say that Gioia went on record as an appreciator of poetry that is musical, comprehensible, and memorizable, while Kleinzahler felt underchallenged by such sentimental, polite, easy-to-read stuff. Fair enough, each to his own, though Kleinzahler's points were blurred by his personal dislike of Keillor, which leaked into his essay like squid ink.

When all was said and done, the debate struck me as being part of the broader argument concerning "accessible" poetry, a modifier so overused that it has begun to have the aural effect of fingernails on a blackboard to my ears. Cited repeatedly in book blurbs, "accessible" has become a praise word used loosely to mean poetry that can be readily understood. The trouble with using the term so broadly is that it can apply equally to the collected works of Mother Goose as well as to many of the poems of Mary Oliver, Sharon Olds, and Philip Larkin. Not to mention Hardy, Coleridge, and Anne Bradstreet. In a more helpful application of the term, I would suggest, "accessible" would mean "easy to enter," like a building. An accessible poem has a clear entrance, a front door through which the reader may pass into the body of the poem whose overall "accessibility"—i.e., availability of meaning—remains to be seen and may vary widely. This more restricted use of the word would remove it from the stone-throwing argument between the camp of Clarity and the camp of Difficulty and require those combatants to come up with more specific and illuminating terms. After all, we may not be able to concur on the aesthetic worth of an architectural structure, but we can all agree that the building is either open or locked.

Let us look at a few examples, as randomly chosen as possible. Here are the opening lines of an *accessible* poem, which happens to be a villanelle:

> We roll up rugs and strip the beds by rote,
> summer expires as it has done before.
> The ferry is no simple pleasure boat . . .
> —*Linda Pastan, "Leaving the Island"*

Here is another:

> After every war
> someone has to clean up.
> Things won't
> straighten themselves up, after all.
> —*Wisława Szymborska, "The End and the Beginning"*

Here is how an *inaccessible* poem begins:

> Streamline to instantaneous
> voucher in / voucher out
> system.
> —*Rae Armantrout, "Up to Speed"*

Or try:

> This begins the chapter pronounced "creation."
>> Here speaks a purple tissue
>> fulminated.
>> Organ, not alive, but somewhat
>>> upward, yeasty from the growing rift.
> —*Elizabeth Robinson, "Tenets of Roots and Trouble"*

These handpicked examples may seem too starkly opposed, but in the real world of reading poetry, when we open a book of poems or happen upon a poem in a magazine, doesn't our first impression include the information that we are either being welcomed or not? Some poems talk to us; others want us to witness an act of literary experimentation. Both *Poetry 180* and *Good Poems*, though assembled according to different methods and criteria, share a preference for the former, poems that are hospitable toward their readers, poems in which a human voice is clearly sounded—poems with the front door left open. If you need to cut an entrance into a poem, who is going to bother? Why should a reader be asked to commit repeated acts of breaking and entering?

As the anthologizer, I tended to choose "accessible" poems, as defined above, not because I wanted to gather into this bouquet only poems that are easy to consume and make few or no demands on the reader. My preference has more to do with the pleasure that is to be derived from a poem's power to convey a reader from one place to another, its capacity for imaginative travel. My question is: If a poem has no clear starting place, how can it go anywhere? If a poem does not begin in lucidity, how can it advance into the mysterious?

The Szymborska poem is a mild example of this kind of travel. A meditation on the aftermath of war—the cleanup, as it's blithely called these days—the poem moves gradually into a future when "All the cameras have left / for another war" and beyond that to the next generation to whom the war means nothing, those who are "starting to mill about / who will find it dull." The poem then steps into a future when grass, as in Whitman, "has overgrown / causes and effects." The poem ends with the image of a fellow reclining on that amnesiac grass, innocent of history, a "blade of grass in his mouth, / gazing at the clouds." Thus the poem, through a series of chronological steps, moves from the rubble of war to the image of a romantic daydreamer, unconsciously enjoying the pastoral calm that is available only in times of peace. It's a simple instance of a poem that operates as a conveyance—here, from the real to the imagined, from history to vision; but again, if the reader is not given a clear starting point, how can he be transported anywhere? If the reader is not oriented at the beginning, how can he be pleasurably disoriented at the end? Or, to use Viktor Shklovsky's terms, how can the reader experience defamiliarization if the familiar is not first offered as a gate of departure?

So much for the scarlet A-word. Now to the collection at hand.

Poetry 180 began as an initiative to introduce clear, contemporary poems into the nation's high schools. A website was posted through the Library of Congress featuring 180 poems—one for every day of the school year—with the hope that a poem would be read each day at the end of the public announcements ("Field hockey tryouts are at 3:30. The yearbook committee meets at 4, and here is the poem for the day"). The idea was to bring students up-to-date by exposing them to the sounds of today's poetry (Sharon Olds not Longfellow, Ron Padgett not William Cullen Bryant) and to show them that poetry could be a feature of everyday life in addition to being a part of their official curriculum. I wanted to make available to students a sample of poems they would be unlikely to come across in a literature textbook or a school-approved anthology. Such books tend to trail woefully behind the leading edge of today's writing. As it turned out, the responses to the website were far more enthusiastic and widespread than I could have imagined. The website continues to average over a million hits a month; hundreds of high schools—

not only from the United States but from Algeria, Bhutan, and Norway, to name a few unanticipated countries—have indicated their participation by registering in the site's guestbook; and the anecdotal buzz continues to be loud. Prompted by the website's success, Random House published a print version of the program in 2003 called *Poetry 180: A Turning Back to Poetry,* aimed at a much broader audience. *180 More: Extraordinary Poems for Every Day* continues the idea of gathering in one place a fresh collection of contemporary poems that both welcomes the reader and provides some of the special pleasures of poetry—irony, feeling, drama, and wordplay, not to mention imaginative thrills.

The deeper hope behind all of these "180" manifestations is that the poems might bring back to poetry those readers who have lost interest or who have had the poetry scared out of them by bad teaching or the wrong menu of poems to choose from. Ideally, the poems under the "180" heading will act as an introduction to the broader world of poetry. I had hoped that curious readers (with or without the help of a teacher) would be guided by these poems to others outside the collection. I envisioned a reader who happened to be struck by a Mary Oliver poem advancing from there to the nature poems of, say, Robinson Jeffers or Pablo Neruda, then to Hopkins and Wordsworth. This type of "branching," as it has been called, invites readers to find their own way in poetry by discovering patterns of influence and association by which poets are connected to other poets, one leaf leading to another. So, instead of the once traditional method of approaching poetry chronologically, which in my schooldays meant beginning with the daunting Middle English of Chaucer, readers would use as a starting place some of the more palatable types of contemporary poetry (you hold 180 of them in your hands) and work backward along lines or branches of influence and commonality. Perhaps a reader who appreciates the humor of David Kirby or James Tate would follow this branch back to Philip Larkin, then to Swift, and maybe—years later—to Chaucer himself.

Apart from any educational value the "180" collections may have, they can be viewed more simply as expressions of my taste in poetry. The anthologizer might be modest enough to leave himself out of the anthology, but the fingerprints of his preferences, however idiosyncratic, are all over every page. After reading many hundreds of poems for this book—and stopping before finishing the vast majority of them—let me mention a few elements that keep me reading a poem. In addition to its shape on the page, a poem makes its first impression with its title. Some titles act as valets ushering us into the poem; others stand guard as if a reader's participation would contaminate the experience. "Abandon All Hope" would be a good generic title for such poems. I have a weakness for ironically provocative titles such as "You Can Change Your Life Through Psychic Power" (James Tate); "I Need to Be More French. Or Japanese." (Beth Ann Fennelly); "Mr. Dithers Explains It All to You" (David Kirby); or "Girls, Look Out for Todd Bernstein" (Jason Bredle). They remind me of some of the great instructive titles of the past: Thomas Gray's "Ode: On the Death of a Favorite Cat Drowned in a Tub of Goldfishes"; Charlotte Smith's "On Being Cautioned Against Walking on an Headland Overlooking the Sea, Because It Was Frequented by a Lunatic"; and, a favorite of many, Lu Yu's "In a Boat on a Summer Evening I Heard the Cry of a Waterbird. It Was Very Sad and Seemed to Be Saying My Woman Is Cruel. Moved, I Wrote This

Poem." I tend to be impatient with cryptic, closed-fist headings like "37 Shards" or "The quarry (1-13)."

I like poems that have a speculative feel to them rather than poems that seem to have their minds already made up. I prefer poems that give the impression that the poem has not been thought out yet and that the poet is feeling his or her way through the poem along with the reader. Poems that proceed tentatively are more likely to provide surprises for the poet as well as the reader. When I hear Kim Addonizio begin her poem "Chicken" with the question "Why did she cross the road?" I trust she doesn't have an answer up her sleeve. Instead, many paths open up, as they do in Robert Minhinnick's opening to "The Fox in the National Museum of Wales" (another grabby title): "He scans the frames but doesn't stop, / this fox who has come to the museum today." Such poems begin with the light-handed feel of the hypothetical, the mode of wonder, the tone of an open investigation.

I am partial to poems that start out as naturally as a conversation might begin, as when Franz Wright opens with "One of the few pleasures of writing / is the thought of one's book in the hands of a kind-hearted / intelligent person somewhere." Or take Darcie Dennigan's awkwardly catchy gambit: "There was this bar in Boston they were in." Poems that start with odd premises also snag my interest: "Reading Hemingway makes me so hungry, / for *jambon,* cheeses, and a dry white wine" (James Cummins) or "Tell me it's wrong the scarlet nails my son sports or the toy store rings he clusters four jewels to each finger" (Victoria Redel). And I am easily seduced by poems that sound like they are up to some mischief:

> I warrant that this
> poem is entirely my
> own work and that
> the underlying ideas
> concepts, and make-up
> of the poem have not
> been taken from any
> other source or any
> other poem but rather
> originate with this poem.
> —*Charles Bernstein, "Warrant"*

I get the same wary feeling from Philip Memmer's "Knowl-edge": "My philosopher friend is explaining again / that the bottle of well-chilled beer in my hand / might not be a bottle of beer . . ." "Well-chilled" perfectly connects the speaker to a world of sensory pleasure immune to the assaults of philosophy.

All of these opening strategies make for truly accessible poetry, but what really counts is what happens once the reader has been ushered inside. Less easy to demonstrate here are the various maneuvers many of these poems execute on their way to unexpected, often eye-opening endings. The lyric poem, however modest in length, is an imaginative vehicle that can transport readers from one zone to another, slipping from dimension to dimension. Thus each poem can be a ride from a place we recognize to a place beyond definition—from a glass ashtray on a table to the mountain of ashes that is the past.

I have lately begun to think of the ideally shaped poem in the way I think of an eye chart. On the top line is the big E, which everyone can plainly see (the chart's "accessibility"), but as we read down, eventually we will come to a line whose legibility is beyond the limits of our vision. Thus, the best poems begin in clarity and end in mystery; they begin with the obvious and then move toward realms of inscrutability where the truth can be approached only by gesture. If every line in a poem were equally clear (all E's), we would be deprived of the ambiguities and secrets that poetry has always been the best means of exploring; if every line were illegible, we would have no ground to stand on, no place from which to view the great riddle at the heart of our existence.

In the preface to his earliest collection of poems, Wordsworth mentions the word "pleasure" over fifty times. And after all the gab and theorizing about poetry (see above), literary hedonism is finally the best motivation to read it. There is no arguing in matters of taste, goes the old saw, but these 180 poems have been assembled based on their willingness to deliver immediate injections of pleasure. Any strong poem should be worth rereading, too—dozens of times in some famous cases—but that is another pleasure, which will apply here as each reader sees fit.

So dig in anywhere. Move from front to back or back to front. Flip the pages. It makes no difference. Here are 180 open doors. Walk right in. And if you hear the click of a door closing behind you, well, that's all part of the kick.

ACKNOWLEDGMENTS

Many people assisted in the work of compiling this collection. My thanks to all the people at the Library of Congress who created the original website (www.loc.gov/poetry/180) and who continue dutifully to maintain it. Thanks to the supporting cast at Random House: Julia Cheiffetz, my dedicated and steadfast editor on this project, who did the hard work of securing permissions (along with Deborah Foley, Tessa Shanks, and Matt Kellogg) and guided the book into print; publicist Jynne Martin for spreading good news to the world; to Dan Menaker for his intelligent overseeing and blessing of the project, and to Gina Centrello, whom I have long been happy to have in my corner. Much of the searching for these poems was done at Poets House in New York, an invaluable resource. Grateful thanks, of course, are due to all the contributors and their publishers, who agreed to accept a nominal permissions fee—something in the mid two-figures. And a tip of the hat is due to George Green for his many helpful suggestions. Finally, continued gratitude goes to my friend Chris Calhoun for his sage companionship and, as always, to Diane, tireless reader, font of approval.

180 *more*

Sharon Olds

That hour, I was most myself. I had shrugged
my mother slowly off, I lay there
taking my first breaths, as if
the air of the room was blowing me
like a bubble. All I had to do
was go out along the line of my gaze and back,
out and back, on gravity's silk, the
pressure of the air a caress, smelling on my
self her creamy blood. The air
was softly touching my skin and tongue,
entering me and drawing forth the little
sighs I did not know as mine.
I was not afraid. I lay in the quiet
and looked, and did the wordless thought,
my mind was getting its oxygen
direct, the rich mix by mouth.
I hated no one. I gazed and gazed,
and everything was interesting, I was
free, not yet in love, I did not
belong to anyone, I had drunk
no milk, yet—no one had
my heart. I was not very human. I did not
know there was anyone else. I lay
like a god, for an hour, then they came for me,
and took me to my mother.

Greg Delanty

I'm back again scrutinising the Milky Way
   of your ultrasound, scanning the dark
      matter, the nothingness, that now the heads say
   is chockablock with quarks & squarks,
gravitons & gravitini, photons & photinos. Our sprout,

who art there inside the spacecraft
   of your ma, the time capsule of this printout,
      hurling & whirling towards us, it's all daft
   on this earth. Our alien who art in the heavens,
our Martian, our little green man, we're anxious

to make contact, to ask divers questions
   about the heavendom you hail from, to discuss
      the whole shebang of the beginning&end,
   the pre-big-bang untime before you forget the why
and lie of thy first place. And, our friend,

to say Welcome, that we mean no harm, we'd die
   for you even, that we pray you're not here
      to subdue us, that we'd put away
   our ray guns, missiles, attitude and share
our world with you, little big head, if only you stay.

Kevin Young

MUZAK | 003

When old, do not let me bark
at passersby—let me be

like the slow motion, down-
the-street dog, ignoring

the cardinals, the colors
he cannot see, even us

as we tiptoe by—
Friend, please save me

from being the neighbors'
fool hound who woofs loud

at every grey squirrel, stray
noise, or lab rushing past

to meet some lady—from being
that cur who cannot help but howl

all night like newlyweds
keeping the world awake. O terrible

angel of the elevator, the plane,
insufferable unquiet we pray to, afraid—

Please make me mild

Because a woman had eaten something
when a man told her not to. Because the man
who told her not to had made her
from another man's bones. That's why
men badgered the heart-side of her chest,
knowing she could not give the bone back, knowing
she would always owe them that one bone.

And you could see how older girls who knew
their catechism armed themselves against it:
with the pike end of teasing combs
they scabbarded in pocketbooks that clashed
against the jumper's nightwatch plaid.
In the girl's bathroom, you watched them
wield the spike in dangerous proximity to their eyes,

shepherding the bangs through which they peered
like cheetahs in an upside-downward-growing grass.
Then they'd mouth the words to "Runaway"
while they ran white lipstick round their lips,
white to announce they had no blood
so any wound would leave no trace, as Eve's
having nothing more to lose must have made

. . .

her fearless. What was weird was how soon
the ordinary days started running past them
like a river, how willingly they entered it
and how they rose up on the other side. Tamed,
or god no . . . your *mother*: ready to settle
with whoever found the bone under her blouse
and give it over, and make a life out of the getting
     back.

W. S. Merwin

And in the morning you are up again
with the way leading through you for a while
longer if the wind is motionless when
the cars reach where the asphalt ends a mile
or so below the main road and the wave
you rise into is different every time
and you are one with it until you have
made your way up to the top of your climb
and brightened in that moment of that day
and then you turn as when you rose before
in fire or wind from the ends of the earth
to pause here and you seem to drift away
on into nothing to lie down once more
until another breath brings you to birth

Naomi Shihab Nye

For the wind no one expected

For the boy who does not know the answer

For the graceful handle I found in a field
attached to nothing
pray it is universally applicable

For our tracks which disappear
the moment we leave them

For the face peering through the cafe window
as we sip our soup

For cheerful American classrooms sparkling
with crisp colored alphabets
happy cat posters
the cage of the guinea pig
the dog with division flying out of his tail
and the classrooms of our cousins
on the other side of the earth
how solemn they are
how gray or green or plain
how there is nothing dangling
nothing striped or polka-dotted or cheery

no self-portraits or visions of cupids
and in these rooms the students raise their hands
and learn the stories of the world

For library books in alphabetical order
and family businesses that failed
and the house with the boarded windows
and the gap in the middle of a sentence
and the envelope we keep mailing ourselves

For every hopeful morning given and given
and every future rough edge
and every afternoon
turning over in its sleep

Kenneth Koch

How lucky that I ran into you
When everything was possible
For my legs and arms, and with hope in my heart
And so happy to see any woman—
O woman! O my twentieth year!
Basking in you, you
Oasis from both growing and decay
Fantastic unheard of nine- or ten-year oasis
A palm tree, hey! And then another
And another—and water!
I'm still very impressed by you. Whither,
Midst falling decades, have you gone? Oh in what lucky fellow,
Unsure of himself, upset, and unemployable
For the moment in any case, do you live now?
From my window I drop a nickel
By mistake. With
You I race down to get it
But I find there on
The street instead, a good friend,
X— N—, who says to me
Kenneth do you have a minute?
And I say yes! I am in my twenties!
I have plenty of time! In you I marry,
In you I first go to France; I make my best friends
In you, and a few enemies. I

Write a lot and am living all the time
And thinking about living. I loved to frequent you
After my teens and before my thirties.
You three together in a bar
I always preferred you because you were midmost
Most lustrous apparently strongest
Although now that I look back on you
What part have you played?
You never, ever, were stingy.
What you gave me you gave whole
But as for telling
Me how best to use it
You weren't a genius at that.
Twenties, my soul
Is yours for the asking
You know that, if you ever come back.

Katia Kapovich

The last time I ran hurdles I showed up
early for the competition. There was still
snow on the Kishinev stadium. Three or four workers
were sweeping it from the tracks.
I took off my coat and dress in a dim locker room
and put on my blue shorts and a white
race jersey with a well-worn number three
printed in red over my chest. Then the other girls
began to arrive, smelling of snow.
Natasha had a strong body and long legs.
When she removed her hair clasp, her blond hair
fell like a mane over her bare shoulder-blades.
Ira, a Tatar girl, was dark and had jet-black eyes.
I knew she was the best in spite of her short stature.
Even Olga, an absent-minded freckled dawdler,
had better chances than I at sixteen.
I left my eyeglasses in the locker and came out
to stretch and warm up before the final race.

Our skin crawling in the cold, white vapor at our nostrils,
ponytails . . . We looked at each other one last time
at the start, before turning into four racehorses.
The pistol awakened us, startling every nerve.
Each step was taut but light-footed. Our elastic ligaments

and warm muscles hurled us through cold winter air.
Clearing hurdle after hurdle, we knew no gravity.

When it was over I looked around and saw the others.
They were behind me. Strangely enough,
it didn't matter to me any longer.

We were tired, and our shoulder-bags felt heavy
as we walked to the bus stop, trotting on ice,
making small talk under our umbrellas.
That Moldovan February was drizzly,
but it was getting warmer toward noon.
The next summer I moved to another city
to study literature.
Are they still running through snow behind me?

Beth Ann Fennelly

I NEED TO BE MORE FRENCH.
OR JAPANESE. | 009

Then I wouldn't prefer the California wine,
its big sugar, big fruit rolling down my tongue,
a cornucopia spilled across a tacky tablecloth.
I'd prefer the French, its smoke and rot.
Said Cézanne: *Le mond—c'est terrible!*
Which means, *The world—it bites the big weenie.*
People sound smarter in French.
The Japanese prefer the crescent moon to the full,
prefer the rose before it blooms.
Oh, I have been to the temples of Kyoto,
I have stood on the Pont Neuf, and my eyes,
they drank it in, but my taste buds
shuffled along in the beer line at Wrigley Field.
It was the day they gave out foam fingers.
I hereby pledge to wear more gray, less yellow
of the beaks of baby mockingbirds,
that huge yellow yawping open on wobbly necks,
trusting something yummy will be dropped inside,
soon. I hereby pledge to be reserved.
When the French designer learned
I didn't like her mockups for my book cover,
she sniffed, *They're not for everyone. They're*
subtle. What area code is 662 anyway? I said,
Mississippi, sweetheart. Bet you couldn't find it

with a map. Okay: I didn't really. But so what
if I'm subtle as May in Mississippi, my nose
in the wine-bowl of this magnolia bloom, so what
if I'm mellow as the punch-drunk bee.
If I were Japanese I'd write about magnolias
in March, how tonal, each bud long as a pencil,
sheathed in celadon suede, jutting from a cluster
of glossy leaves. I'd end the poem before anything
bloomed, end with rain swelling the buds
and the sheaths bursting, then falling to the grass
like a fairy's castoff slippers, like candy wrappers,
like spent firecrackers. Yes, my poem
would end there, spent firecrackers.
If I were French, I'd capture post-peak, in July,
the petals floppy, creased brown with age,
the stamens naked, stripped of yellow filaments.
The bees lazy now, bungling the ballet, thinking
for the first time about October. If I were French,
I'd prefer this, end with the red-tipped filaments
scattered on the scorched brown grass,
and my poem would incite the sophisticated,
the French and the Japanese readers—
because the filaments look like matchsticks,
and it's matchsticks, we all know, that start the fire.

Leanne O'Sullivan

The day the doctors and nurses are having
their weekly patient interviews, I sit waiting
my turn outside the office, my back to the wall,
legs curled up under my chin, playing

with the hem of my white hospital gown.
They have taken everything they thought
should be taken—my clothes, my books,
my music, as if being stripped of these

were part of the cure, like removing the sheath
from a blade that has slaughtered.
They said, Wait a few days, and if you're good
you can have your things back. They'd taken

my journal, my word made flesh, and I think
of those doctors knowing me naked,
holding me by my spine, two fingers
under my neck, the way you would hold a baby,

taking my soul from between my ribs
and leafing through the pages of my thoughts,
as if they were reading my palms,
and my name beneath them like a confession,

• • •

owning this girl, claiming this world
of blackness and lightness and death
and birth. It lies in their hands like a life-line,
and I feel myself fall open or apart.

They hear my voice as they read
and think, Who is this girl that is speaking?
I know the end, she tells them.
It is the last line, both source and closing.

It is what oceans sing to, how the sun moves,
a place for the map-maker to begin.
Behind the door, nothing is said.
Like dreams, my clothes come out of their boxes.

Alan Michael Parker

Too young for her body's changes

but ready anyway, the angle of
her teen years practiced every night

watching TV from the plush sofa, one hand dangling—
she knows just how to try on

the fishnet, body-hugging, full-length red sweater

as she steps from the dressing room
of the thrift store, met by her mother's panic:
Mama, can I have it please?

And oh, how I want Mama to say yes,
and oh, how I want Mama to say no,

because how can you choose?

And which body will be
my next body, within this life?

(It isn't you, I tell the mirror,
and put back the porkpie hat.)

• • •

Behind the register a gaggle of figurines,
blind beneath their fezzes,
beams upon us all—

glazed thrift shoppers, the odd lot,
gleeful and desperate.

What brightly painted doodads,
what riches on the racks,

and oh, the girl and the four dollar red sweater!

She's still a little girl, middle school
three weeks away and an hour's
bumpy bus ride in the summer rain,

wending down the coastal highway:
she'll listen to her Mama.

Me? I'll listen to the rain
typing gibberish on my umbrella,
and try trying on

word after word after word,

. . .

always getting wrong the color of the rosehips
along the muddy ditch, a blurred swath of
pink and green by the thrift store sign,

wedged in the present,

where a little girl twirls a shopping bag
and stomps in every puddle in the parking lot.

Mary Jo Salter

Once, in a doorway in Paris, I saw
the most beautiful couple in the world.
They were each the single most beautiful thing in the world.
She would have been sixteen, perhaps; he twenty.
Their skin was the same shade of black: like a shiny Steinway.
And they stood there like the four-legged instrument
of a passion so grand one could barely imagine them
ever working, or eating, or reading a magazine.
Even they could hardly believe it.
Her hands gripped his belt loops, as they found each other's
    eyes,
because beauty like this must be held onto,
could easily run away on the power
of his long, lean thighs; or the tiny feet of her laughter.
I thought: now I will write a poem
set in a doorway on the Boulevard du Montparnasse,
in which the brutishness of time
rates only a mention; I will say simply
that if either one should ever love another,
a greater beauty shall not be the cause.

Kenneth Koch

Where did you come from, lamentable quality?
Before I had a life you were about to ruin my life.
The mystery of this stays with me.
"Don't brood about things," my elders said.
I hadn't any other experience of enemies from inside.
They were all from outside—big boys
Who cursed me and hit me; motorists; falling trees.
All these you were as bad as, yet inside. When I spoke, you were
    there.
I could avoid you by singing or by acting.
I acted in school plays but was no good at singing.
Immediately after the play you were there again.
You ruined the cast party.
You were not a sign of confidence.
You were not a sign of manliness.
You were stronger than good luck and bad; you survived them
    both.
You were slowly edged out of my throat by psychoanalysis
You who had been brought in, it seems, like a hired thug
To beat up both sides and distract them
From the main issue: oedipal love. You were horrible!
Tell them, now that you're back in your thug country,
That you don't have to be so rough next time you're called in
But can be milder and have the same effect—unhappiness and
    pain.

Suzanne Cleary

The woman pushes a grocery cart
flanked by four daughters, nine to fifteen,
all shades of blond, grey-eyed, slender,
swings a bag of apples into the cart,
as if accompanied by her younger selves
who, having followed her and led her through the aisles
now stand, for a moment, close behind her

like the imaginary painting entitled "Trick Pear"
(remarkable for its size alone, 8" × 80"),
one Anjou pear in each of five separate panels,
the same pear from five different angles
one very productive afternoon of painting

followed by weeks of indecision
as to which pears to keep, to frame,
how to frame, until, easily,
for no discernable reason, the painter understood
they must be framed together, side by side
by side, to suggest the many in one, posed

like Muybridge's men and women stripped bare
for the studies of human locomotion,
especially like the dark-haired woman
who drops the white scarf, stoops

to pick it up, drops the scarf, scoops
it up again, as if she has just found it,

just seen it for the first time,
as the painter, staring at the pear,
has to see it freshly, freshly again.

She painted almost as if she could not name the fruit—
as someone in the middle of love-making
will feel her mouth open and, out of habit or loss,
think to speak, almost speak except that her lover
touches her lips with a finger that welcomes silence back,
that makes of the entire body a mouth—

and so the painter in the process of painting
does not name the pear, nor its colors,
nor the gradations and valences of rose,
orange, chartreuse, the pear's blush and patina
changing as the light changes in her studio
above the kitchen, the narrow yard,

February, late afternoon, on a day lit by snow,
by her brush moving first toward the ideal pear
on the blank canvas, next, the day lit
by her finding, instead, this other pear,

lumpy, mottled, actual, a model
endlessly patient and cooperative,

finding too this canvas pear or pears
(time will tell her how to think of this)
whereupon light speaks to paint,
paint speaks to light, and to paint,
almost as if the painter has dissolved
except for those times she steps back

and stares at her work, presses the handle of her brush
against her lip, and thinks,
for this process is not divorced from thought.
It is deep thought, this playing with the facts
of the perfect pair: the ideal pear
and this actual pear, perfect because it is here,

simply here on the blue cloth thrown as if
casually over the scratched brown table,
this pear available to her in the middle of winter
as if miraculously, although actually here

due to refrigerators and trains and trucks,
not to mention the hands that picked it,
as if miraculously, although actually here

due to refrigerators and trains and trucks,
not to mention the hands that picked it,

someone else who labored at midday,
after the sugars had risen through the woody stem.
As she paints, she already, in some part
of her mind or her body, knows she will frame
the pear or pears in apple wood sanded smooth as butter,
and as she glances at the work table

on which four canvas pears wait,
she almost sees these five should be in one frame,
that someday people will debate,
"Is it five pears, or one?" Someone
will go to great length to prove her untitled painting one,
possibly dancing, pear, a trick pear

but she cannot be distracted, she keeps painting,
working and reworking until she grows hungry,
and works a bit beyond that, dusk seeming to pause,
to hold off its ripening, all of her selves working beside her
as she touches the fruit with her brush,
and lifts it.

Kate Bass

When I know you are coming home
I put on this necklace:
glass beads on a silken thread,
a blue that used to match my eyes.
I like to think I am remembering you.
I like to think you don't forget.

The necklace lies heavy on my skin,
it clatters when I reach down
to lift my screaming child.
I swing her, roll her in my arms until she forgets.
The beads glitter in the flicker of a TV set
as I sit her on my lap
and wish away the afternoon.

I wait until I hear a gate latch lift
the turn of key in lock.
I sit amongst toys and unwashed clothes,
I sit and she fingers the beads until you speak
in a voice that no longer seems familiar, only strange.
I turn as our child tugs at the string.
I hear a snap and a sound like falling rain.

Frederick Morgan

From our corner window
rainy winter mornings
we watch the yellow school busses
nudging their way down Park
moistly glowing, puddled by the rain.

Stopping at doorways here and there
where children climb aboard
they merge into the traffic's flow
and dwindle from our sight.

We watch—then turn away,
and when in changing light
we look again, we see a stream
dark and serene in China,
down which sleek goldfish dart and gleam.

Tell me it's wrong the scarlet nails my son sports or the toy
    store rings he clusters four jewels to each finger.

He's bedecked. I see the other mothers looking at the star
    choker, the rhinestone strand he fastens over a sock.
Sometimes I help him find sparkle clip-ons when he says
    sticker earrings look too fake.

Tell me I should teach him it's wrong to love the glitter that a
    boy's only a boy who'd love a truck with a remote that revs,
battery slamming into corners or Hot Wheels loop-de-looping
    off tracks into the tub.

Then tell me it's fine—really—maybe even a good thing—a boy
    who's got some girl to him,
and I'm right for the days he wears a pink shirt on the seesaw in
    the park.

Tell me what you need to tell me but keep far away from my son
    who still loves a beautiful thing not for what it means—
this way or that—but for the way facets set off prisms and
    prisms spin up everywhere

and from his own jeweled body he's cast rainbows—made every
   shining true color.

Now try to tell me—man or woman—your heart was ever once
   that brave.

Christopher Howell

DINNER OUT | 018

We went to either the Canton Grill
or the Chinese Village, both of them
on Eighty-second among the car lots
and discount stores and small nests
of people waiting hopelessly
for the bus. I preferred the Canton
for its black and bright red sign
with the dragon leaping out of it
and sneezing little pillows of smoke.
And inside, the beautiful green
half-shell booths, glittery brass encrusted
lamps swinging above them.

What would I have?
Sweet and sour?
Chow mein with little wagon wheel-shaped
slices of okra and those crinkly noodles
my father called deep fried worms?
Fried rice?

Among such succulence, what did it matter?
We could eat 'til we were glad and full, the whole
family sighing with the pleasure of it.
And then the tea!
All of this for about six bucks, total,

my father, for that once-in-a-while, feeling
flush in the glow of our happy faces
and asking me, "How you doing, son?"

Fine, Dad. Great, really, in the light
of that place, almost tasting
the salt and bean paste and molasses, nearly
hearing the sound of the car door
opening before we climbed in together
and drove and drove,
though we hadn't far to go.

Cecilia Woloch

All the quick children have gone inside, called
by their mothers to *hurry-up-wash-your-hands*
honey-dinner's-getting-cold, just-wait-till-your-father-gets-
     home—
and only the slow children out on the lawns, marking off
paths between fireflies, making soft little sounds with their
     mouths, *ohs*
that glow and go out and glow. And their slow mothers
     flickering,
pale in the dusk, watching them turn in the gentle air, watching
     them
twirling, their arms spread wide, thinking, *These are my*
     children, thinking,
Where is their dinner? Where has their father gone?

Paul Muldoon

They remember Gene Chandler topping the charts with "Duke
    of Earl"
when the boys were set on taking the milk bar's one banquette
and winning their hearts, Mavis and Merle,

as it seemed their hearts might be first to yield,
hearts before minds. Time for stilettos. Time for spivs with shivs.
The time of day when light fails on the field

while their daughters, themselves now tweenie girls,
crowd round a coach for one last tête-à-tête.
They remember Gene Chandler topping the charts with "Duke
    of Earl"

while the world still reeled
from the anti-Castro Cubans going to sea in a sieve,
as it seemed. Their hearts might be first to yield

if only after forty years of one plain, one purl,
on the sweater they've sweated over for a Bay of Pigs vet,
and winning their hearts, Mavis and Merle,

may now be faintly likelier for a well-heeled
schlub to whom they once wouldn't so much as give
the time of day. When light fails on the field

. . .

a schlubster linesman will unfurl
an offside flag that signals some vague threat,
they remember. Gene Chandler topping the charts with "Duke
 of Earl"

for three weeks only in 1962 might have taught them to shield
themselves against the lives their daughters briefly relive,
as it seemed *their* hearts might be first to yield

to this free kick that forever curls
past the goal mouth, a ball at once winging into the back of the
 net
and winning. Their hearts, Mavis and Merle,

hanker for the time when it was not yet revealed
failure's no less literal than figurative,
the time of day when light fails on the field

and gives back a sky more muddy than mother-of-pearl,
so it's with a deepening sense of regret
they remember Gene Chandler topping the charts with "Duke
 of Earl"
and winning their hearts, Mavis and Merle.

Jim Daniels

What are you going to do
when your girlfriend's pregnant
neither of you have health
insurance or a decent job
and you've both been taking enough
drugs to kill a horse
or two?

What are you going to do
when she calls up from Wisconsin
three states away to tell you
she's pregnant, that she slipped
away the night before

she's telling you
and she's crying and she's telling you
she's going to the clinic
in the morning?

You know.
You know what you're going to do.
You're going to drive
your Plymouth Satellite all night
. . .

your head jangling
like the coins you use to call her
from rest stops to make sure
she'll wait
wait till you get there

drive all night to her sister's
in Madison and sit with her in the morning
wringing your hands and going over it
all again, slowly, and again

and you can't let yourself
think for more than a second
of the actual child
you might have together,
what you imagined while driving
when the cold air and darkness
when the lack of a radio
made all things possible

you kiss her and hold her
and wipe her nose
and wipe your nose
and you try to ignore
and not feel embarrassed by

the presence of her sister
silently circling the house.

What do you do? You drive her down
in the painful sun, the forced
squint, you pull out the wrinkled
wad of bills you conned
from friends half-gone in the bar,
you lick your fingers,
you count out your half.

George Bilgere

for my marriage, 1996–2000

I want a good night's sleep.
I want to get up without feeling
That to waken is to plunge through a trap door.

I want to ride my motorcycle
In late spring through the Elysian Fields
Of the Rocky Mountains

And lie once more with Cecelia
In the summer of 1985
On a blanket in the backyard of our house

In Denver and watch the clouds expand.
And it would be great to see my mother
Alive again, at the stove, frying a pan of noodles

Into that peculiar carbonized disk that has never been replicated.
I would like for my ex-wife to get leprosy,
Her beauty falling away in little chunks

To the disgust of everyone in the chic café
Where she exercises her gift
For doing absolutely nothing.

. . .

I want world peace.
I want to come home one evening
And find that Julia, the new assistant professor

In the history department,
Has let herself into my apartment
For the express purpose of lecturing me

On the history of lingerie.
I don't ask for much: a good merlot.
An afternoon thunderstorm cooling off

The city as I sit listening to Ella
Sing "Spring is Here," so the air goes lyrical
And perhaps a stray bolt of lightning

Strikes my ex-wife as she steps from her car,
Setting her on fire, to the unqualified delight
Of the friends she has come to visit,

Who are thoroughly sick of her self-aggrandizing stories
I want to spark a bowl of Maui Wowie
And spend the entire afternoon in my dorm room

. . .

With Corrine Spellman, trying to remember
What we were talking about, wondering
Whether, in fact, we had had sex yet.

I'd like to sit at the little outdoor restaurant
By the lake in Forest Park, talking with my aunt
In the humid summer twilight, as the hot

St. Louis day expires upon the water
And the moth-eaten Chinese lanterns
Glow like faded Kodachrome.

We would argue about the great tenor voices
Of the century, or causes for the dearth
Of poetry about the Gulf War,

Or why my father drank himself into an elegy
We never stop revising,
While couples on their paddleboats come in

From the darkening lake, as they've done
Since the beginning of time, and children
Call each other across the shadowy fields.

• • •

Yes, that would be nice.
I want a good woman
With a sweet bosom

And a wicked sense of humor.
I want to wake up in London on a spring morning
And read in the paper that my ex-wife

Has received a lethal injection, courtesy of the state
Of Ohio, as part of a citywide program aimed
At improving the civic pride of Cleveland,

But something went terribly wrong
And she's been left in a persistent
Vegetative state

Which everyone agrees
Is nonetheless an improvement.
And it would be wonderful

To sit down with Maria
At our favorite restaurant in Madrid
With some good red wine
• • •

And listen to her Spanish
Caress the evening.
I want to read that a new manuscript

Of poetry by James Wright
Has been discovered in someone's attic,
And someone I haven't yet met,

In some future I have yet to despoil,
Has bought it for my birthday,
And after the kids are asleep

We sit out in the backyard,
A little drunk, and read it
Aloud to each other,

Something we often do
In summer, before climbing upstairs to the bedroom
In the big old house we love so much.

Douglas Goetsch

I pay bills the way he did,
checkbook, calculator, roll
of stamps laid out on a Sunday
near the end of the month,
ripping the perforations, stuffing
the trash can with what doesn't matter,
licking envelopes, a tidy stack
of outgoing mail, adding it up
to get the number for the month
which keeps the walls around me.
Maybe he felt powerful, or just
responsible, signing those checks,

sitting hours at his desk, slumped,
his big back to me and the rest
of the house. What I did
was bring him coffee, black
steaming cups burning my fingers
down the long carpeted hallway.
I emptied his ashtray. I put my small
fists in his shoes and shined them.
If there was more to my father
it was in a place I couldn't see,
and now that I'm approaching
the age he was when we stopped

. . .

speaking, I'm beginning to get
a hint of him in what I say
when I'm not thinking, a glimpse
of his hairline in the rear view mirror.
Sometimes on the golf course I imagine
he's golfing too, five states away,
studying his ball, waggling the club
three times the way I do, a signature
twist of the back, left hand
up to shade the eyes, and the same
God damn son of a bitch!
when it disappears into trees.

Kevin Stein

How not to think of love, entering
    Blackbeard's Floral Ship Shoppe
to "Louie, Louie" playing on WMXP

93.3 FM, "All Louie, All the Time,"
    where only a DJ's poorly recorded
sophomorics spell our need for order.

Surely the owners must be out to lunch,
    abandoning their floral ship to a crew
of Gen-Xers in baggy jeans and cropped tops

cranking the ultimate garage band song
    so seductively even the door buzzer
can't be heard above the din, and who

at such moment dances with eyes open?
    The sign says *Ring Bell for Service*
though I won't, having two minutes

to indulge an anthem to pleasures
    only hormone-engorged teenagers
make out amidst the mythic muddle

• • •

shouted into the lone mic strung
>   twelve feet above the drunken Kingsmen:
state of the art recording, circa 1963.

Ah history's got a good beat and you
>   can dance to it, even if you don't know
Richard Berry sold "Louie, Louie" for a mere

$500 bucks to flip side "You Are My Sunshine,"
>   how the tune languished in a Tacoma 10-cent
record bin till Rockin' Robin Roberts reworked

a version the Kingsmen later covered,
>   whose out-of-focus vocals convinced us
the lyrics were obscene; how that rumor shot

the song to *Billboard*'s #2 and led the feds
>   to a padded room to spin the platter
first fast then s-l-o-w enough to conclude

the lyrics were "unintelligible at any speed"—
>   confirming no one over thirty gets it.
An *it* we two swaddled in the thrice-a-week

• • •

sheets of our college bed, beside
     the burnished urn, the cinnamon candles,
incense wreathed above a turntable's

vaulted altar. There we'd bear youth's Grail
     and Bowl, we'd wear the fated talisman.
We'd swear our sweaty vows beneath its

cryptic lyrics, reedy three-cord organ
     so hypnotic even now Blackbeard's
back room letter-stuffers sway like weeds

in the fluorescent wash of its tidal pull.
     Framed by the door's lit portal,
two of them wail "Lou—ee, Lou—I,"

their lips parting sea. They smile, they dance.
     They lick envelopes with rhythmic grace
though the song halts and starts over

for the twentieth time this hour, the plodding
     postmodern irony of *classic rock* lost
among lyrics so malleable you make them

• • •

anything you want. As once, my love,
    you named yourself a garden, braided daisies
in your hair, then sweetly let me in.

Michelle Boisseau

TARIFF | 025

It takes time to appreciate how I once
made a friend so unhappy the next night
on the road from Chauncey to Amesville, Ohio,
she steered her Fiat Spider head on
into an on-coming truck. Her boyfriend
identified her waitress uniform.
She's been dead now for more than twenty years.
What I did to hurt her I won't tell you—
so you're free to imagine any vicious,
self-indulgent, hapless blunder or crime

while I go about turning this into a poem again,
turning over heavy marl, the garden
in spring, and the wind picks up, flinging soil
against my neck, behind my ears, into my teeth.
You have to get dirty: what *appreciate*
means is *to price*. After living a while
you understand the ways you have to pay.

Carol Muske-Dukes

This is your passport I hold in my hand:
a hemisphere, half red ink, half blue—
as yet untorched by terror, but polluted

perhaps by the gaze of the future. For
example, the shadow of the parachute of
my desire, this rip-cord rip of your photo-

blink, your eyes translated into these
flashing sad idioms. Take this blank page
for the remainder, the last boring national

tattoos. *Wave me through* these invisible
brackets of lightning. Stars shatter on
the epaulets of all the uniforms, the hats

and coats of countries that no longer exist.
I wear your insignia, therefore I wear death's
insignia. Which means that nothing can hurt me.

And with these wings and flames, I pledge
allegiance to nothing: I can go anywhere.

Yannis Ritsos

They took the plough to the field,
they brought the field into the house—
an endless interchange shaped
the meaning of things.

The woman changed places with the swallow,
she sat in the swallow's nest on the roof and warbled.
The swallow sat at the woman's loom and wove
stars, birds, flowers, fishing boats, and fish.

If only you knew how beautiful your mouth is
you would kiss me on the eyes that I might not see you.

Translated by Minas Savvas

Michael Donaghy

Dearest, note how these two are alike:
This harpsichord pavane by Purcell
And the racer's twelve-speed bike.

The machinery of grace is always simple.
This chrome trapezoid, one wheel connected
To another of concentric gears,
Which Ptolemy dreamt of and Schwinn perfected,
Is gone. The cyclist, not the cycle, steers.
And in the playing, Purcell's chords are played away.

So this talk, or touch if I were there,
Should work its effortless gadgetry of love,
Like Dante's heaven, and melt into the air.

If it doesn't, of course, I've fallen. So much is chance,
So much agility, desire, and feverish care,
As bicyclists and harpsichordists prove

Who only by moving can balance,
Only by balancing move.

Hugo Williams

Please come late,
so that I have almost given you up
and have started glancing round the room,
thinking everyone is you.
Please don't come
until I have started missing you,
thinking I will never see you again,
praying you are lost.
Come too late for me not to notice.
Make me suffer,
wondering what you are doing
on the other side of town,
still in your dressing down.
make me beg for mercy
when you pick up a magazine.

Are you looking in your mirror,
suddenly remembering me?
I'm on my second coffee by now,
eating the little bits of sugar in my cup.
Haven't you even set out yet?
I decide I don't want to see you after all.
I don't really like you.
I'd rather be on my own.
I know it is all over between us,

but I go on sitting here,
reading a newspaper,
not understanding a word.
If you came in now, I wouldn't recognise you.
Don't come anywhere near me
until I have gone slightly mad for love of you.

David Baker

It is to Emerson I have turned now,
damp February, for he has written
of the moral harmony of nature.
The key to every man is his thought.
But Emerson, half angel, suffers his
dear Ellen's dying only half-consoled
that her lungs shall no more be torn nor her

head scalded by her blood, nor her whole life
suffer from the warfare between the force
& delicacy of her soul & the
weakness of her frame . . . March the 29th,
1832, of an evening strange
with dreaming, he scribbles, I visited
Ellen's tomb & opened the coffin.

—Emerson looking in, clutching his key.
Months of hard freeze have ruptured the wild
fields of Ohio, and burdock is standing
as if stunned by persistent cold wind
or leaning over, as from rough breath.
I have brought my little one, bundled and
gloved, to the lonely place to let her run,

. . .

hoary whiskers, wild fescue, cracks widened
along the ground hard from a winter drought.
I have come out for the first time in weeks
still full of fever, insomnia-fogged,
to track her flags of breath where she's dying
to vanish on the hillsides of bramble
and burr. The seasonal birds—scruff cardinal,

one or two sparrows, something with yellow—
scatter in small explosions of ice.
Emerson, gentle mourner, would be pleased
by the physical crunch of the ground, damp
from the melt, shaped by the shape of his boot,
that half of him who loved the Dunscore heath
too rocky to cultivate, covered thick

with heather, gnarled hawthorn, the yellow furze
not far from Carlyle's homestead where they strolled,
—that half of him for whom nature was thought.
Kate has found things to deepen her horror
for evenings to come, a deer carcass tunneled
by slugs, drilled, and abandoned, a bundle
of bone shards, hoof and hide, hidden by thick

• • •

bramble, or the bramble itself enough
to collapse her dreams, braided like rope, blood-
colored, blood-barbed, tangled as Medusa.

What does she see when she looks at such things?
I do not know what is so wrong with me
that my body has erupted, system
by system sick unto itself. I do

not know what I have done, nor what she thinks
when she turns toward her ill father. How did
Emerson behold of his Ellen, un-
embalmed face fallen in, of her white hands?
Dreams & beasts are two keys by which we are
to find out the secrets of our own natures.
Half angel, Emerson wrestles all night

with his journal, the awful natural
fact of Ellen's death, which must have been
deeper sacrifice than a sacrament.
Where has she gone now, whose laughter comes down
like light snow on the beautiful hills?
Perhaps it is the world that is the matter . . .
—His other half worried by the wording.

Alison Marsh Harding

On highway 5 the moon
is low and bright in the sky, a natural headlight.
It is not the orange globe of my childhood,
when the dish ran away with the spoon,
nor the oyster of last month,
pearlizing my walk through the lily garden.

It is the moon the general talked
about on the radio station Sunday morning,
when he said "the night of the full moon,
is perfect to begin a war."

Now, I imagine the man in the moon
strobing the cannon of light,
across a field of soldiers and dust riddled road,
down the mountain and into the valley,
past abandoned clothes hanging on the line,
to the darkened houses, a blazing guide.

Robert Wrigley

Wearing only moonglow
    and the fire's final shawls of smoke,
she made her way from the tent
    at 2 a.m., then squatted to pee,

and the heavenly light showed me everything:
    its cool tongues of silver lapping mountain
stones and the never-motionless leaves
    of aspens, licking her back, her hips,

haunches, and more, illuminating even the deep
    green eyes of whatever animal it was
that watched her from the forest then—
    a deer, I believed, and still believe,

though I confess I did not rise that night
    to make sure, did not shine my light or murmur
but waited, letting my head
    as she returned settle slowly back

down to the pillow made of my clothes
    and welcomed her shivering
back into the tent, from which
    I had sworn I would not look.

Cathleen Calbert

I know why all the old men want young girls,
why the other old men love young boys,
for I see how they are like the young girls,
having whispered into your ear, my dear,
and stroked your Chatterton pale chest,
the soft bowl of your Botticelli belly.

I know why men leave their old wives,
wives their old husbands, why women love
their men, why women love their women,
for you seem to me masculine, then again
feminine: your almond eyes, smooth cheeks.
I know why mothers do so love their sons,

and daughters their good fathers, and why
a bed is a good, good thing (as are
down pillows, quilts, clean sheets),
why heterosexuals believe they've found
a perfect symmetry of difference, why
homosexuals believe they have found

a perfect balance of mirroring, why
young lovers like to drink too much
and make a drunken, careless love,

why couples always cook so much,
and our lips dip in that slippery curve,
why the rest can seem like nothing more

than a morning lie we tell ourselves
so we will leave our beds and keep
an interest in our professional lives,
why many must make a dangerous love
and threaten these professional lives,
why all lovers will give it one more try,

why we are finally willing to fail,
why we will still let ourselves fall
in love, why I, surely old enough
(a cautious friend kindly implies)
to know better, can think of nothing
better than the buoyancy of your body,

the great gift of your gentleness, how
kind you are, in love with me, and why,
with a spinster's age and weight of sorrow,
in white below the green of your parents'
weeping willows, I will take these vows,
knowing nothing other than our love.

W. S. Di Piero

THE LITTLE FLOWERS | 034

My neighborhood's newest dreamboat
taking his morning coffee. Flip-flops
pajama top, hair screwy from bed—
girls in cupcake pigtails notice
the coy, coltish looks,
but off his meds the atmosphere
clogs up, he says, with goofy dust.
Joy or jaybird panic crushing
his skull, head cocked
at birds not flying past,
smiling up, heaven sunbathing,
loosing love to purplish ethers
in his head, now may-poling
the parking meter a million children
and me in shorts and Keds
round-dancing with him,
then back to mug and book,
tipsy rock-a-bye in his chair,
big head aswish, singing a little
Happy to be loved by you.
Dear stranger, keep it light,
Jim Dandy to the Rescue

or frivolous *fioretti* hymn
to your air of birds not there,
to irrelevant brick and sky,
to the Pacific so close still
not close enough to hear.

Michael Longley

It is as though David had whitewashed the cottage
And the gateposts in the distance for this moment,
The whooper swans' arrival, with you wide awake
In your white night-dress at the erratic boulder
Counting through binoculars. Oh, what day is it
This October? And how many of them are there?

Jane Routh

On your first visit, you put your feet up
on my polished table. Ankles crossed.
Doc Martens. (And this was years after
they were out of fashion with the young.)

It can't have been easy
for a small woman like you
to have kept your feet up like that.
I had to talk to you by leaning round.

I didn't know what to do—
whether to push them off, offer a cushion,
tell you I couldn't see you for your feet,
or ask if you had trouble with circulation.

I did the sort of thing I always do:
I just set a knife on one side
and a fork on the other as if that were
a customary greeting for soles

and kept my face blank.
It must have been a test, because
I never saw you do it again, not here,
not at home, not in a waiting room.

• • •

You came again so many times
I must have passed, though
feel I failed: I still don't know
what you wanted me to do.

Cecilia Woloch

THE HAMMOCK | 037

We've driven all day to get here—
Robert steering the Olds with one hand
from L.A. to San Francisco and now
I'm stretched out in Jorge's hammock
where he left me, on the porch,
having begged me, *Lie down, rest,*
said I looked tired, then came back,
wrapped me in the quilt from his own bed.
No stars tonight, but there are clouds;
I watch them cross the blue-black sky,
just watch and listen—from the kitchen
at my back, men's voices, soft:
Jorge's voice and Robert's voice
and the sounds of chopping,
chopping, talk of vegetables and sex.
I hear them speaking of childhood gardens,
what they ate but did not love
and what they love, and what I love

is just to lie here, listening;
swaying in the hammock
while these clouds go scudding past
and the smell of beans with garlic
wafts out through the open door.
It's the end of summer, the end, I swear,

of my last doomed love affair.
I'll spend this weekend with my friends,
these poets and kissers of my hand,
wine being poured, fog rolling in
across the dark, their voices calm.
Oh men I love, oh men I've never slept with,
calling me to eat.

Rebecca Wee

HEART'S ITCH | 038

a few blossoms, the lowly mountains, that pair in the tunnel of love
—and it is a tunnel, and it is love—

> —*Jane Miller*

We walked, undressed, in a tawny field, and the heat
on my legs where the sun hit, dear god, your voice reeling into
    my ear.
I believe in a source, I do. A soul.

A reason, however unsound. Even nostalgia and its distortions—
in spite of the unmarked graves.

Later, fire-vine stitched over stucco, apples on a white plate,
a freezer clacking with ice.

There *is* something to it, something creaturely, raw,
in the stretch of your spine. Your dear lips.

Tonight fog takes the ravine. An owl amends the quiet.

On a beach a man pushes a cart with his life
through the sand. A shoe, a towel, the tinging of cans.

The moon that scores his face perfects yours.
What are we to make of this?
The sky is filling with black flowers.

. . .

Still, love insists on the ludicrous: nicknames, kissing in the
   street.

My darling, what is it, this mulish faith that wheels and gleams
between us? A trace of headway? Recovery from loss?
That pair of hawks overhead?

Carol Ann Duffy

7 April 1852.
Went to the Zoo.
I said to Him—
Something about that Chimpanzee over there
    reminds me of you.

Theodore Deppe

While my children swim off the breakwater,
while my wife sleeps beside me in the sun,
I recall how you once said you knew
a sure way to paradise or hell.
Years ago, you stood on the Covington bridge,
demanded I throw my coat into the Ohio—
my five dollar "Russian greatcoat,"
my "Dostoevsky coat," with no explanations,
simply because you asked.

From that height, the man-sized coat fell
in slow motion, floated briefly,
one sinking arm bent at the elbow.
At first, I evade the question when my wife asks,
as if just thinking of you were an act of betrayal.
The cigarette I shared with you above the river.
Our entrance into the city, your thin black coat
around both our shoulders. Sometimes I can go
weeks without remembering.

Ricardo Pau-Llosa

SAMURAI | 041

Bruno came up to the girl at the bar
and she was already talking halfway
out of one side of her mouth while, he knew it,
looking at him with one eye at least through the smoke
she dropped everywhere from the chatted cigarette
and the pointed nails, and he knew it was all falling
in place, the look, the lights, the small moves he was
making toward her, the glance this way and that,
and when she said ham on rye to the waiter
he jumped in talking about samurai figuring
that was her thing, her lust right out of history,
dazed her a bit but she kept up her order ignoring
in that flirtatious opposite-of-what-I-really-want
kind of way his prize prey always gave him
despite his more and more on the sword, the layered
steel and the funny knobs of hair that meant all sorts
of things to heroes from back then and look simply
weird to her, no doubt, right? he asked, but I know
better, ham on rye came right by him and he stared
at it as she began to munch it trying harder to ignore
him, and then he finally broke down, Know
all about ham and rye, breed the pig, plough the field,
know all I need to know to get to that chewing.

Darcie Dennigan

There was this bar in Boston they were in.
It was October. The college boys had come back to town.
I was taking a walk when I saw them—five girls

singing "Happy Birthday"—"Happy Birthday to Ella."
Not that I could hear them through the window
from the street. Their singing was like wind through the high
    trees—

I didn't hear the sound—I saw it move across their lip gloss.
The day was Oct. 21st to be exact, feast of Saint Ursula
and Ella's birthday. The story goes that Saint Ursula died

a virgin. Ella probably would not. Ursula led 11,000
virgins to martyrdom. Ella led five girlfriends to a bar
on Beacon Hill. Whether or not anyone at the bar was still

a virgin was not something I could tell from the street.
It was a vagrant's twilight—clear, only just cool, and beds
of oak leaves all over the Common. Ella wore a black v-neck shirt

with a deep neckline. She seemed to feel exposed—she kept
her shoulders rounded for cover. Saint Ursula wore a tunic, I think.
She had no armor either. The other girls wore their shirts black
    and tight,

. . .

tight and black. They didn't really look like virgins.
Not to the college boys shooting darts in the back and squinting
at them under their Cocks, Bulls, Hornets hat brims.

Painters have made Ursula's face pale & resolute—
like a woman in a Titian portrait, only without the flush.
For flush, there were the girls, whose faces were blossoming

with lemon-drop shots—they'd lick the back of their hands,
sprinkle that little saliva patch with sugar, shoot down
a measure of gin, suck a lemon slice, then lap up the sugar.

Fun, though from a distance it looked—well, all that licking
in public—the sugar grits on their black shirts
nothing like stars over a black sea or the city on the suburb's

horizon—just a plain stain, a start of a girl's plain story.
The girls each did three shots in ten minutes. One was a little
    bigger
than the others. She did four shots, all elbows and gusto.

The eleven thousand virgins split up into three ships.
I don't know where all those girls came from. But they were going
to Rome. They had good wind & the going was fast, but

• • •

something happened. Ursula & her virgin army disembarked
in Cologne and smiled at men with dirty hands,
asking them to become Christians. And then an angel appeared

in the high trees, telling Ursula—someday, you'll die here,
you & all your tenderfoot friends—a message Ursula hid
in herself and so sailed on. Sailed on? I was leaning against a
     sapling's

thin, thin trunk. The face of each girl visible over the windowsill.
Each face bright against the bar's dark walls, but nothing like
     stars over
a black sea. I leaned against a sapling, but no angel appeared in
     the high trees.

Because it was October, the sapling was dying. Its leaves looked
beautiful—flushed and resolute. Only, hidden somewhere in
     itself—
maybe in its very thin trunk—was the secret that it was dying.

I didn't know exactly what I was doing there, so I was going
to do it harder. Ursula's face I made the color of wet concrete,
ashy, because of her secret, and because as I stood on the
     sidewalk,

. . .

it began to rain. Ella's face grew redder than ever—an almost
profane red. She was talking to the boys—challenging them
to a round of darts maybe, as one girl chewed her cuticles,

and the bigger girl laughed—it was a loud laugh, and a fake
    one—
I could tell. All five girls had secrets on their complexions.
It was a feast day of secrets. No one knew why Ursula's three
    ships returned

to Cologne. Why the prince of Cologne kissed Ursula's concrete
    cheek
and asked her to marry him. He was a pagan, a Hun. All the
    Hun men
wanted the virgins to sleep with them—on the ground, on
    beds

of oak leaves, I imagined. The virgins refused, and their blood
stained the leaves as they stared ahead, hard—at a god or the
    horizon.
The girls' mothers had told or hinted to them—never go down

on unfamiliar college boys in pub bathrooms. But then two of
    the boys

and two of the girls were gone. I should have prayed then for a god
to reveal her pattern. I didn't pray, though—I don't pray and
    what happens

is, sometimes, the sidewalk space beneath a neon bar sign
    seems to me
a holy station. So I lean against a dying sapling. In a chapel
outside Cologne sits a vault full of girls' bones. The arrow shot

through Ursula's throat by the prince of the Huns sits there too.
As Ella threw her darts, the cross hanging from a string of
    rosary beads
she wore as a belt around her jeans would sway side to side.
    Maybe that was

my imagination. All that's certain about Ursula is a Latin
    inscription,
ten lines by Clematius, etched into a rock. And then legend,
    and darkness.
There was something there about Ursula and her love of the
    faith.

And near annihilation: a fabulous heap of the gleaming pelvic
bones of virgins. But Ella lived in neither chaste nor epic days.
Ella loved only bright windows against dark streets. Or not—

. . .

that was more me. Ella was playing darts and doing shots.
    Sometime
after "Happy Birthday," after the bathroom groping, one dart
    went astray
and pegged her exposed collarbone. Then some of the boys
    went home

with some of the girls. One girl went home alone. The dart
    thrower
brought Ella to an ER for a tetanus shot, for a bandage,
for his love of the skin around her collarbone. Their artifacts:
    torn

wrapping paper; a thin, profanely red ribbon, scored and
    curled;
sucked lemon wedges. A waitress cleared it all away. For the
    love
of the faith of bright windows, I stayed outside, looking

for the pattern. Fact after girl after virgin fact. It had been
a vagrant's twilight. Now the streetlights were turning the
    sidewalks
into islands. Everything looked like stars over a black sea.
    Everything

. . .

seemed to be dying. From my holy station, I had kissed each
    artifact
and still did not see the secret. Then the bar shut down. Boston
had a curfew. Bright windows died early. After that, if you were
    still trying

to look in, you'd see just your reflection. I gave a halo to the
    sapling.
Made some girls saints and the alley, a black sea. Sorry mom,
    god,
you there, I said, out loud, I need to make love to something.

C. K. Williams

Although he's apparently the youngest (his little rasta-beard is
    barely down and feathers),
most casually connected (he hardly glances at the girl he's with,
    though she might be his wife),
half-sloshed (or more than half) on picnic-whiskey teen-aged
    father, when his little son,
two or so, tumbles from the slide, hard enough to scare
    himself, hard enough to make him cry,
really cry, not partly cry, not pretend the fright for what must
    be some scarce attention,
but really let it out, let loudly be revealed the fear of having
    been so close to real fear,
he, the father, knows just how quickly he should pick the child
    up, then how firmly hold it,
fit its head into the muscled socket of his shoulder, rub its
    back, croon and whisper to it,
and finally pull away a little, about a head's length, looking, still
    concerned, into its eyes,
then smiling, broadly, brightly, as though something had been
    shared, something of importance,
not dreadful, or not very, not at least now that it's past, but
    rather something . . . funny,
funny, yes, it was funny, wasn't it, to fall and cry like that,
    though one certainly can understand,

we've all had glimpses of a premonition of the anguish out
    there, you're better now, though,
aren't you, why don't you go back and try again, I'll watch you,
    maybe have another drink,
yes, my son, my love, I'll go back and be myself now, you go be
    the person you are, too.

Ron Koertge

History of the Royal Society

It's 1667. Reason is everywhere, saving
for the future, ordering a small glass of wine.
Cause, arm in arm with Effect, strolls by
in sturdy shoes.

Of course, there are those who venture
out under cover of darkness to buy a bag
of metaphors or even some personification
from Italy, primo and uncut.

But for the most part, poets like Roderigo
stroll the boulevards in their normal hats.
When he thinks of his beloved, he opens
his notebook with a flourish.

"Your lips," he writes, "are like
lips."

Jen? Hi, it's Dorie. I'm on the bus to LaGuardia. . . . Atlanta.
What?. . . Maybe. I'm not really sure. I mean his schedule is so
        whacked,
y'know? . . . But anyway. I was telling you about Marcie. Yeah.
        So
I said to her, I said, Marcie, this one seems different, y'know?
I said the last few guys you've dated—from what you've told
        me—
I mean frankly—. . . Yeah. I said, Marcie, they might be
like very charming, y'know, and with great jobs, but frankly—
what it comes down to is, Let's hit the bed,
and in the morning, Thanks for the excellent coffee. Y'know?
But this guy—. . . What? It's Jason. Yeah.
So I said Marcie, from what you've said, Jason sounds
        different—
and from what Bob said about him also. . . . Bob knows him
from some project last fall. So I said Marcie, you've had, what,
two coffees, two lunches, and a *dinner*, and he still hasn't—. . .
No, Bob says he's definitely straight. . . .
I think there was a divorce like six years ago or something. But
        my—
What? . . . That's right, yeah, I did. At Nathan's party after some
        show. . . .
Yeah, "The Duchess of Malfi," I forgot I told you. What? . . .

Only for five minutes—one cigarette, y'know? . . . Kind of low-
    key,
like thoughtful. But my point is—. . . Yeah, exactly! So I said,
Marcie, this is a guy who understands, y'know,
that bed is like *part* of something, y'know?
Like it's not the big *objective* for godsake. It's like an *aspect*—
What? . . . Exactly—it's an *expression* of something much more—
Yes!—it's like, Can we be companions in *life*, y'know?
So I said, Marcie, for godsake—if you don't give this guy
like a serious chance, somebody else—y'know? . . . Right,
I mean let's face it—. . . Jen? I'm losing you here—am I breaking
    up?
Jen, I'll call you from the airport—Okay bye.

Jason Bredle

Because after sitting out for a spell
he's back with a degree in accounting and a high
paying position in one of the leading pharma-
ceutical corporations in the country
and the aspirations of owning that exotic
yellow sports car, license plate
EVIL. And like Dennis Meng at Sycamore
Chevrolet stakes his reputation
on his fully reconditioned used cars,
I stake my reputation on telling you
Todd Bernstein means business this time,
girls. No more of this being passed
over for abusive alcoholic football
stars. He's got a velour shirt now.
No more of your excuses—if he wants you,
you're there. None of this I'm washing
my hair Friday night nonsense—come on,
you think Todd Bernstein's going to fall
for that? He knows you're not studying, not
busy working on some local political
campaign, not having the guy who played
Cockroach on *The Cosby Show* over
for dinner, not writing any great American
novel. He's seen your stuff for God's sake,

and it's simply nothing more than mediocre,
long prose poems with titles like
"The Falling" and "Crucible" and "Waking
to Death" that force impossible metaphors,
despairing about love and womanhood
and how bad your life is even though
you grew up happily in suburban America,
or at least as happily as anyone can grow up
in suburban America, which normally, you know,
consists of the appearance of happiness while
your dad is doing three secretaries
on the side and your mom pretends not to know
and brags to the entire town about how you're
an actor about to star in a sitcom about the mis-
adventures of a cable TV repairperson
who, while out on a routine installation
one day accidentally electrically blasts
herself into the living room of a family
of barbarian warlords on a planet near
Alpha Centauri who force her into slavery
before sending her on a pillage mission
to a planet of cloxnors who capture her
and place her in a torture institution
where she meets a vulnerable meeb whom

she convinces, because of her cable TV
repairperson skills, to let her become nanny
to its impressionable meeblets just before
it's about to rip off her limbs with its ferocious
abnons and devour her. The results,
according to your mom, are hilarious, but
come on, you and I both know the story is
just so *predictable*. And Todd knows damn well
your writing doesn't pull off
any metaphors for the happiness that was
taken from you by some dude who played
the guitar and called himself a musician
when all he could really do was play
a couple of chords and sing about true love
and alligators and how the alligator
represents true love which somehow
explains why somebody cut open
an alligator one time in Florida
to find a golfer. There's just no fooling
Todd. Sure, he'll act like he's interested,
that's Todd Bernstein, and he'll make
remote claims that he too has written
or been artistic at some point in his life,
but Todd Bernstein knows all you girls
really want is a piece of good old

Todd Bernstein. No longer will any
strange auras enter the bedroom
during sex and keep him from maintaining
an erection, no longer will any women
walk out on him repulsed. If anybody's
walking out after sex, it'll be
Todd Bernstein, I can assure you.
He won't be humiliating himself by falling
down a flight of stairs in front of a group
of Japanese tourists anymore, but rather
coaxing entire groups of women into his bed-
room. Because that's Todd Bernstein. He's on
the move. And he wants you to know, girls,
that he's well aware *you certainly can't learn*
Korean sitting around here which is why
he's out there right now, preparing
for the slew of women just beyond his sexual
horizon, spray-painting GIRLS, LOOK OUT
FOR TODD BERNSTEIN on the side
of a Village Pantry.

What am I to you now that you are no
longer what you used to be to me?

Who are we to each other now that
there is no us, now that what we once

were is divided into me and you
who are not one but two separate and

unrelated persons except for that ex-
that goes in front of the words

that used to mean me, used to mean
you, words we rarely used (husband, wife)

as when we once posed (so young and helpless)
with our hands (yours, mine) clasped on the knife

that was sinking into the tall white cake.
All that sweetness, the layers of one thing

and then another, and then one thing again.

J. Allyn Rosser

BEFORE THE SICKNESS
IS OFFICIAL | 048

I bring you a book I've always wanted to read.
I don't think you know yet that I know.
I don't bring photographs.
I don't bring flowers that will die in your azure vase
on the cool marble table.
I don't bring potted plants that will live
a long long time.
I give you a slightly twisted smile
and you give it right back.
Want some wine?
I drink beer instead.
My words come out unwieldy
with the weight of other words.

Everything in your apartment is so clean,
as if you were expecting some other guest.

You bring me the new sketches
which ostensibly I came here to see
and I take your time looking at them.
You take a phone call in the kitchen,
where your voice assumes a new business-
likeness, distant and rehearsed.

• • •

I lift a paperweight and put it back
exactly where it was.

You carry your wine back into the room
with your pale, strong-boned fingers.
We compete in cracking the pistachios
that don't have openings, giving points
for neatness of shell and wholeness of nut.
The nuts are in a crimson bowl
you made in ninth grade.
The sketches are inchoate but good.
I tell you they're good.
I tell you they're really good.
You pause and give me a chance to bring it up.
I pause too. I say it's late.
You give me back my coat, its pockets
full of keys to my future car,
my future office, my future apartments
shared with friends I don't yet know.
As I leave, you joke briefly about
your thinning hair: *Parting is such sweet sorrow.*
Then you say something else
I won't be able to recall.

Leanne O'Sullivan

Driving to my doctor in July, I sit
with my feet on the dashboard, calves
glinting in the white heat, a new lexicon
crawling around the corners of a napkin

as I try to write against my thighs. Above
our red Toyota the branches and leaves
of Ireland have kindled with the sky,
a Monet where there was once a Cézanne.

My mother seeks out the straightest routes,
allows the car to ebb the smooth middle
of the road as the wind laps the rim
of the window, staccato to the music

of Cat Stevens. I think she loves
the passion of overtaking, the thunder
of engines flirting on opposite sides
of the road. The corners of her eyes

will sharpen. Her stomach will tense
and flatten. Lips taut, she takes the reins
of our lives with both hands,
and as I close my eyes she delivers me

• • •

to the darkness just before birth, the pulse
of gears aroused, swelling, like the hum
induced by speed. We slide along the vein
of Mom's road, our bodies moving through

the air like seeds through a pistil, and when
I can feel my hair whipping my jaw again
I open my eyes and glance at my mother,
strands of her hair tucking in the salty tattoo

of the wind, her elbow angling over the lip
of the door. We descend, sending loose chips
flying like progress. She drives faster and faster
as if she's driving to save my life. We're falling

through the green of Ireland and Mom has
the gear-stick in her fist, as if it's the strong
branch of a tree to cling to. I change stations
on the radio, touching her fingers.

Lynne McMahon

Common all over Ireland, unknown to me,
    (tell me again the name of this thing?)
it's a *claddagh*, a sweetheart ring,
    silver hands clasping a rounded heart,
an apple, I mistakenly thought,
    topped by a crown.
I still think of it as my regnant *pomme*
    because it's French, and wrong,
and invented etymologies pass the time
    those days you're gone.
Irish clichés, like certain songs,
    wring from me
a momentary recognition that trash
    sent bowling down the street
by sudden wind, or showery smoke trees
    whipsawing across the path
their fine debris, means home to me,
    and however long
estranged we've been, or silvered over
    by borrowed themes,
these homely things make meaning of us.
    I feel it just as much as you—
that near-empty diner in Sligo
    where you found the ring

wedged in the cushioned booth,
        rejected, perhaps, or lost,
hidden while the lover nervously rehearsed
        his lines, then abruptly interrupted,
who knows how, and now distraught,
        had no more thought for such
sentiment as this. I never take it off.

Lynn Powell

The radio's replaying last night's winners
and the gratitude of the glamorous,
everyone thanking everybody for making everything
so possible, until I want to shush
the faucet, dry my hands, join in right here
at the cluttered podium of the sink, and thank

my mother for teaching me the true meaning of okra,
my children for putting back the growl in hunger,
my husband, *primo uomo* of dinner, for not
begrudging me this starring role—

without all of them, I know this soup
would not be here tonight.

And let me just add that I could not
have made it without the marrow bone, that blood-
brother to the broth, and the tomatoes
who opened up their hearts, and the self-effacing limas,
the blonde sorority of corn, the cayenne
and oregano who dashed in
in the nick of time.

Special thanks, as always, to the salt
you know who you are—and to the knife,

who revealed the ripe beneath the rind,
the clean truth underneath the dirty peel.

—I hope I've not forgotten anyone—
oh, yes, to the celery and the parsnip,
those bit players only there to swell the scene,
let me just say: sometimes I know exactly how you feel.

But not tonight, not when it's all
coming to something and the heat is on and
I'm basking in another round
of blue applause.

Sharon Olds

She was four, he was one, it was raining, we had colds,
we had been in the apartment two weeks straight,
I grabbed her to keep her from shoving him over on his
face, again, and when I had her wrist
in my grasp I compressed it, fiercely, for almost a
second, to make an impression on her,
to hurt her, our beloved firstborn, I even nearly
savored the stinging sensation of the squeezing, the
expression, into her, of my anger,
"Never, never again," the righteous
chant accompanying the clasp. It happened very
fast—grab, crush, crush,
crush, release—and at the first extra
force, she swung her head, as if checking
who this was, and looked at me,
and saw me—yes, this was her mom,
her mom was doing this. Her dark,
deeply open eyes took me
in, she knew me, in the shock of the moment
she learned me. This was her mother, one of the
two whom she most loved, the two
who loved her most, near the source of love
was this.

Margaret Atwood

VARIATION ON THE
WORD *SLEEP* | 053

I would like to watch you sleeping,
which may not happen.
I would like to watch you,
sleeping. I would like to sleep
with you, to enter
your sleep as its smooth dark wave
slides over my head

and walk with you through that lucent
wavering forest of bluegreen leaves
with its watery sun & three moons
towards the cave where you must descend,
towards your worst fear

I would like to give you the silver
branch, the small white flower, the one
word that will protect you
from the grief at the center
of your dream, from the grief
at the center. I would like to follow
you up the long stairway
again & become
the boat that would row you back
carefully, a flame

in two cupped hands
to where your body lies
beside me, and you enter
it as easily as breathing in

I would like to be the air
that inhabits you for a moment
only. I would like to be that unnoticed
& that necessary

Margaret Levine

I must have been about six.
We had just arrived from Canada.
Every day I missed Paulette
and Larry the frog.
I wanted my ant farm back.
All I had was the blue elephant
and a few marbles.
On the other side of the hill
near our house, I knew
I would find Prince Edward Island again.
It was getting cold.
I had a cap gun and a doughnut with me.

Norman MacCaig

When a clatter came,
it was horses crossing the ford.
When the air creaked, it was
a lapwing seeing us off the premises
of its private marsh. A snuffling puff
ten yards from the boat was the tide blocking and
unblocking a hole in a rock.
When the black drums rolled, it was water
falling sixty feet into itself.

When the door
scraped shut, it was the end
of all the sounds there are.

You left me
beside the quietest fire in the world.

I thought I was hurt in my pride only,
forgetting that,
when you plunge your hand in freezing water,
you feel
a bangle of ice round your wrist
before the whole hand goes numb.

Czeslaw Milosz

ENCOUNTER | 056

We were riding through frozen fields in a wagon at dawn.
A red wing rose in the darkness.

And suddenly a hare ran across the road.
One of us pointed to it with his hand.

That was long ago. Today neither of them is alive,
Not the hare, nor the man who made the gesture.

O my love, where are they, where are they going
The flash of a hand, streak of movement, rustle of pebbles.
I ask not out of sorrow, but in wonder.

Translated by Czeslaw Milosz and Lillian Vallee

Dick Davis

A MONORHYME FOR
THE SHOWER | 057

Lifting her arms to soap her hair
Her pretty breasts respond—and there
The movement of that buoyant pair
Is like a spell to make me swear
Twenty-odd years have turned to air;
Now she's the girl I didn't dare
Approach, ask out, much less declare
My love to, mired in young despair.

Childbearing, rows, domestic care—
All the prosaic wear and tear
That constitute the life we share—
Slip from her beautiful and bare
Bright body as, made half aware
Of my quick surreptitious stare,
She wrings the water from her hair
And turning smiles to see me there.

Ted Kooser

A pattern of curly acanthus leaves,
and woven into one corner
in blue block letters half an inch tall:
MADE FROM WOOL FROM SHEEP
KILLED BY DOGS. 1778.
As it is with jacquards,
the design reverses to gray on blue
when you turn it over,
and the words run backward
into the past. The rest of the story
lies somewhere between one side
and the other, woven into
the plane where the colors reverse:
the circling dogs, the terrified sheep,
the meadow stippled with blood,
and the weaver by lamplight
feeding what wool she was able to save
into the faintly bleating, barking loom.

Elizabeth Macklin

In the tropical glass of a cool, foreign
mirror, I saw myself for the first time:
head forward on my unstraightened spine
from too much reading, cheeks scored

by impatience. I can never control
my eyes—gray, saddened at will,
with an uncurbed glare for looked-for double-dealing,
but still looking half a simpleton's after all.

And then, where the surface wavered,
I saw surprise—a sweating older woman, her coming
printed in faint lines around my mouth—and loved
the old bitch, whole, as if she were my next-door neighbor.

Edward Hirsch

Today I am pulling on a green wool sweater
and walking across the park in a dusky snowfall.

The trees stand like twenty-seven prophets in a field,
each a station in a pilgrimage—silent, pondering.

Blue flakes of light falling across their bodies
are the ciphers of a secret, an occultation.

I will examine their leaves as pages in a text
and consider the bookish pigeons, students of winter.

I will kneel on the track of a vanquished squirrel
and stare into a blank pond for the figure of Sophia.

I shall begin scouring the sky for signs
as if my whole future were constellated upon it.

I will walk home alone with the deep alone,
a disciple of shadows, in praise of the mysteries.

Harvey Shapiro

NATIONAL COLD STORAGE
COMPANY | 061

The National Cold Storage Company contains
More things than you can dream of.
Hard by the Brooklyn Bridge it stands
In a litter of freight cars,
Tugs to one side; the other, the traffic
Of the Long Island Expressway.
I myself have dropped into it in seven years
Midnight tossings, plans for escape, the shakes.
Add this to the national total—
Grant's tomb, the Civil War, Arlington,
The young President dead.
Above the warehouse and beneath the stars
The poets creep on the harp of the Bridge.
But see,
They fall into the National Cold Storage Company
One by one. The wind off the river is too cold,
Or the times too rough, or the Bridge
Is not a harp at all. Or maybe
A monstrous birth inside the warehouse
Must be fed by everything—ships, poems,
Stars, all the years of our lives.

Katia Kapovich

PAINTING A ROOM | 062

for Irina Kendall

Here on a March day in '89
I blanch the ceiling and walls with bluish lime.
Drop cloths and old newspapers hide
the hardwood floors. All my furniture has been sold,
or given away to bohemian friends.
There is nothing to eat but bread and wine.

An immigration visa in my pocket, I paint
the small apartment where I've lived for ten years.
Taking a break around 4 p.m.,
I sit on the last chair in the empty kitchen,
smoke a cigarette and wipe my tears
with the sleeve of my old pullover.
I am free from regrets but not from pain.

Ten years of fears, unrequited loves, odd jobs,
of night phone calls. Now they've disconnected the line.
I drop the ashes in the sink, pour turpentine
into a jar, stirring with a spatula. My heart throbs
in my right palm when I pick up the brush again.

For ten years the window's turquoise square
has held my eyes in its simple frame.

Now, face to face with the darkening sky,
what more can I say to the glass but thanks
for being transparent, seamless, wide
and stretching perspective across the size
of the visible.

Then I wash the brushes and turn off the light.
This is my last night before moving abroad.
I lie down on the floor, a rolled-up coat
under my head. This is the last night.
Freedom smells of a freshly painted room,
of wooden floors swept with a willow broom,
and of stale raisin bread.

It's 2 a.m. and I can't remember
the last name of my friend Joy
who died of breast cancer.
I can see her wig, slightly matted,
with the curls she always wanted,
see her holding hands with her daughter
that afternoon we walked to Long Point.
But the name . . . a *W*, I think . . . damn it . . .
Joy, who kicked her drinking husband out
the last month, who interviewed
the local politician (*no sir, tell me*
what you think, not what you think
everyone wants you to think),
who drew a thousand yellow smiley faces
and called it *Portraits of Prozac.*
Walton? Williams? Winston?
I brought her copies of *Vanity Fair* and *People,*
heated a few cans of tomato soup
in her grease-splattered kitchen.
I never took an SOS pad to that back-splash
or made a homemade stew, never
drove her, like her good neighbor did,
to the Grand Canyon, i.v. trolley in tow.
I just sat with her every few weeks
in that dark bedroom that smelled

of her daughter's new kittens,
picked up her spilled blue pills
from the carpet under her bed and ticked them
one by one into the bottle,
reaching for them the way I'm combing my mind
now for her name: Wilson? Wiggins?
The tattered paisley address book
is gone so I can't look her up
and anyone who knew her is asleep now
so I can't call—and besides,
my stepdaughter is downstairs talking
to a boyfriend an ocean away,
which is how far I feel from late-night
hushed giggles and a phone cord
stretched to the front stoop,
that is how old I am now, old enough
to have forgotten the name of a friend
who died, *died* for God's sake,
not a friend who gave me a ride
to Syracuse one weekend or loaned me
a gown for a college ball.
Her daughter lives with the ex now.
He's remarried and sober, I'm told.
Once when my husband and son
ran out of gas on Route 213,

the new wife picked them up in her red Saab
and took them to the Texaco in Galena.
She seems nice, they said. Dyes her hair.
Gwinner. Joy Gwinner. And her daughter's name
is Hope.

Stephen Dobyns

At the edge of a golf course, a man watches
geese land on a pond, the bottom of which
is spotted with white golf balls. It is October
and the geese pause in their long flight.

Honking and flapping at one another, they seem
to discuss their travels and the man thinks
how the world must look when viewed from above:
villages and cornfields, the autumn trees.

The man wonders how his own house must look
seen from the sky: the grass he has cut
a thousand times, the border of white flowers,
the house where he walks from room to room,

his children gone, his wife with her own life.
Although he knows the geese's honkings are only
crude warnings and greetings, the man also
imagines they tell the histories of the people

they travel over, their loneliness, the lives
of those who can't change their places, who
each year grow more isolated and desperate.
Is this what quickens his breathing when at night

. . .

the distant honking seems mixed with the light
of distant stars? Follow us, follow us, they call,
as if life could be made better by departure,
or if he were still young enough to think it so.

Daniel Lusk

UNDERSTUDY | 065

Old men who eat alone in small cafes
arrange the silver carefully
beside the plate.

It crawls inside their cuffs
and edges out again along their temples
and the gothic arches of their brows.

Arranging is the life
now
isn't it.

Old men check their watches
frequently,
lest the sand run out unnoticed
onto the table by the water glass.

Their hands flutter
over the fork and spoon again, the knife,
as if the knife were a lost opportunity
or a love that might be set to rights.

Attentive as they are to these
small handles,
I suspect if they let go

• • •

they'll belly up with loneliness
and float off toward the ceiling fans
in all these small cafes

where I sit watching, hours on end,
to learn their little order,
eating alone.

Edward Nobles

POPULAR MECHANICS | o66

I pull her panties to the floor
    and hold them there
against the floorboards. The measured
    lines widen and
close, though all along to the wall
    each is exact–
ly two inches from the other;
    the carpenter
saw to that. In the distance, small

      clouds of dust
    accumulate beneath the bed; they
      glide along, slowly pushed
by an invisible gust, until they
hesitate at an iron leg. The cloth
    is blue—I remember
it—white cotton on the inner pouch.
      The chair legs

      catch the light
from the window and hold it. In one
    I can see the entire
circumference of the sun. A red yellow
marble rolls through the dust and stops at
    a penny. The elastic

band contorts and expands. The cloth is
    soft. Under

    the dresser,
the bent corners of a magazine.
    Popular Mechanics?
Probably, with colored photos. The floor-
boards are greyed, cold. It is still winter. The
    hot cloth plays dead. I look
up at the sky outside the window.
    The small clouds

of dust accumulate beneath
    the bed. I hold
tight, then begin to slide—slowly,
    not moving, up-
ward, outward, into space. I hes-
    itate a few
years at an iron leg, then move
    on, wondering
at the blackness, the exactness
    of the measured line.

Alice Fulton

If you believe you would have caressed every lash
and freckle that I was
but for decorum, I appreciate the thought.
Have you ever been embarrassed
by a frugal kiss? It is embarrassing to live.

My love for my husband was all balled up
with mothering. I had compassion for any flesh
trying that hard to be iron. Imagine
living with his bluster and hiss
for forty years. Have you ever been embarrassed
by a frugal kiss? I died of it. Just say I sublimed.
Snowflakes do this all the time. Say I was tired
of eating beige, for heaven's sake. Of
molestations imposed by my own body.
Let's see. I wasn't stoical enough for me.

You might say I've eased into the trees
and the autistic fields: eyes like forget-me-
nots. "Desire." All that business you admire.
The human yen for angels is depraved.
It decorates death with heaven, longing
for the note I never left.

• • •

My last sound was like the small release
of strings and frets you sense
when a guitarist changes chords.
Enough to let you know the music's made by hand.

I am not without regrets,
picayune as they may seem or plain
grotesque. I do regret the writing.
I wanted to be self-reliant.
I wanted to reach up and shut
my own eyes just before I died.

Julie Sheehan

I hate you truly. Truly I do.
Everything about me hates everything about you.
The flick of my wrist hates you.
The way I hold my pencil hates you.
The sound made by my tiniest bones were they trapped in the
    jaws of a moray eel hates you.
Each corpuscle singing in its capillary hates you.

Look out! Fore! I hate you.

The little blue-green speck of sock lint I'm trying to dig from
    under my third toenail, left foot, hates you.
The history of this keychain hates you.
My sigh in the background as you pick out the cashews hates you.
The goldfish of my genius hates you.
My aorta hates you. Also my ancestors.

A closed window is both a closed window and an obvious
    symbol of how I hate you.

My voice curt as a hairshirt: hate.
My hesitation when you invite me for a drive: hate.
My pleasant "good morning": hate.
You know how when I'm sleepy I nuzzle my head under your
    arm? Hate.

The whites of my target-eyes articulate hate. My wit practices it.
My breasts relaxing in their holster from morning to night hate
    you.
Layers of hate, a parfait.
Hours after our latest row, brandishing the sharp glee of hate,
I dissect you cell by cell, so that I might hate each one
    individually and at leisure.
My lungs, duplicitous twins, expand with the utter validity of
    my hate, which can never have enough of you,
Breathlessly, like two idealists in a broken submarine.

Robert Wrigley

She's twelve and she's asking the dog,
who does, but who speaks
in tongues, whose feints and gyrations
are themselves parts of speech.

They're on the back porch
and I don't really mean to be taking this in
but once I've heard I can't stop listening. Again
and again she asks, and the good dog

sits and wiggles, leaps and licks.
Imagine never asking. Imagine why:
so sure you wouldn't dare, or couldn't care
less. I wonder if the dog's guileless brown eyes

can lie, if the perfect canine lack of abstractions
might not be a bit like the picture books
she "read" as a child, before her parents' lips
shaped the daily miracle of speech

and kisses, and the words were not lead
and weighed only air, and did not mean
so meanly. "Do you love me?" she says
and says, until the dog, sensing perhaps

• • •

its own awful speechlessness, tries to bolt,
but she holds it by the collar and will not
let go, until, having come closer,
I hear the rest of it. I hear it all.

She's got the dog's furry jowls in her hands,
she's speaking precisely
into its laid-back, quivering ears:
"Say it," she hisses, "say it to me."

Stephen Dobyns

Party all day, party all night—a man
wakes up on the floor of a friend's kitchen.
It's still dark. He can hear people snoring.
He reaches out and touches long silky hair.
He thinks it's his friend's daughter. Actually,
it's a collie dog. He can't see a thing
without his glasses. He embraces the dog.
Why is the daughter wearing a fur coat?
He gropes around for the daughter's breasts
but can't find them. The dog licks his face.
So that's how it's going to be, is it?
The man licks the collie dog back. He tries
to take off his pants but gets his underwear
caught in the zipper, so they only smooch.
He tells the collie dog about his wife,
how they only make love once a month.
He tells the collie dog about his two sons,
how they have robbed him blind and ruined
the record player. The dog licks his face.
The man tells the collie dog that he loves her.
He decides in the morning he and the daughter
will run away and immigrate to New Zealand.
They will raise sheep and children. Each evening
as the sun sets they will embrace on their

front porch with a deep sense of accomplishment.
He will stop drinking and playing cards.
The man falls asleep with the image of
the little log house clearly before his eyes.
When he wakes in the morning, he finds
the collie dog curled up beside him. You bitch,
he cries, and kicks her out of the kitchen.
He staggers off to find the daughter's bedroom.
Time to leave for New Zealand, my precious.
The daughter screams. The father comes running,
grabs his friend, and throws him out of the house.
Later the father has lunch with a priest.
He describes how this fat old clerk had tried
to rape his daughter. Was it drugs, whiskey,
or general depravity? They both wonder at
the world's approaching collapse. Sometimes
at night the father starts awake as if
he'd missed a step and was suddenly falling.
Where am I? he asks. What am I doing?
The waitress brings them coffee. The father
can't take his eyes off her. He forgets
what he was thinking. She has breasts the size
of his head. He wants to take off his shoes
and run back and forth across her naked body.
Let us leave him with his preoccupation.

Like an airborne camera, the eye of the poem
lifts and lifts until the two men are only
two dark shapes seated at the round table
of an outdoor cafe. The season is autumn.
The street is full of cars. It is cloudy.
This is the world where Socrates was born;
where Jesse James was shot in the back
as he reached up to straighten a picture;
where a fat old clerk prowls the streets,
staring into the face of every dog he meets,
seeking out the features of his own true love.

Greg Delanty

FROM WOODY'S RESTAURANT, MIDDLEBURY | 071

Today, noon, a young macho friendly waiter and three diners,
    business types—two males, one female—
are in a quandary about the name of the duck paddling
    Otter Creek,
the duck being brown, but too large to be a female mallard.
    They really
want to know, and I'm the human-watcher behind the nook
    of my table,
camouflaged by my stillness and nonchalant plumage.
    They really want to know.
This sighting I record in the back of my *Field Guide to People.*

F. J. Bergmann

Forgive me
for backing over
and smashing
your red wheelbarrow.

It was raining
and the rear wiper
does not work on
my new plum-colored SUV.

I am also sorry
about the white
chickens.

Don McKay

Bill Evans Solo Sessions 1963

To find your way through the
phrase. Some keys are made of edges some
of broken glass. Bauble. Bangle. You knew the tune
before it was mined. You are the kind of fool
who searches through the rubble of his favourite
things. A note could fall in love off
a cliff down a well. When you fall it
will be forever. Whoever has no house whoever
picks his way and finds
his favourite ledge. Far from April,
far from Paris. Far from his left hand down there
pecking the bright shiny beads. Telling them
off. That kind of fool. Everything
happened to you.

Lawrence Raab

WHY IT OFTEN RAINS IN
THE MOVIES | 074

Because so much consequential thinking
happens in the rain. A steady mist
to recall departures, a bitter downpour
for betrayal. As if the first thing
a man wants to do when he learns his wife
is sleeping with his best friend, and has been
for years, the very first thing
is *not* to make a drink, and drink it,
and make another, but to walk outside
into bad weather. It's true
that the way we look doesn't always
reveal our feelings. Which is a problem
for the movies. And why somebody has to smash
a mirror, for example, to show he's angry
and full of self-hate, whereas actual people
rarely do this. And rarely sit on benches
in the pouring rain to weep. Is he wondering
why he didn't see it long ago? Is he wondering
if in fact he did, and lied to himself?
And perhaps she also saw the many ways
he'd allowed himself to be deceived. In this city
it will rain all night. So the three of them
return to their houses, and the wife
and her lover go upstairs to bed

while the husband takes a small black pistol
from a drawer, turns it over in his hands,
then puts it back. Thus demonstrating
his inability to respond to passion
with passion. But we don't want him
to shoot his wife, or his friend, or himself.
And we've begun to suspect
that none of this is going to work out,
that we'll leave the theater feeling
vaguely cheated, just as the movie,
turning away from the husband's sorrow,
leaves him to be a man who must continue,
day after day, to walk outside into the rain,
outside and back again, since now there can be
nowhere in this world for him to rest.

Laurel Blossom

FIGHT | 075

That is the difference between me and you.
You pack an umbrella, #30 sun goo
And a red flannel shirt. That's not what I do.

I put the top down as soon as we arrive.
The temperature's trying to pass fifty-five.
I'm freezing but at least I'm alive.

Nothing on earth can diminish my glee.
This is Florida, Florida, land of euphoria,
Florida in the highest degree.

You dig in the garden. I swim in the pool.
I like to wear cotton. You like to wear wool.
You're always hot. I'm usually cool.

You want to get married. I want to be free.
You don't seem to mind that we disagree.
And that is the difference between you and me.

Donna Masini

I watched a snake once, swallow a rabbit.
Fourth grade, the reptile zoo
the rabbit stiff, nose in, bits of litter stuck to its fur,

its head clenched in the wide
jaws of the snake, the snake
sucking it down its long throat.

All throat that snake—I couldn't tell
where the throat ended, the body
began. I remember the glass

case, the way that snake
took its time (all the girls, groaning, shrieking
but weren't we amazed, fascinated,

saying we couldn't look, but looking, weren't we
held there, weren't we
imagining—what were we imagining?).

Mrs. Peterson urged us to *move on girls*,
but we couldn't move. It was like
watching a fern unfurl, a minute

• • •

hand move across a clock. I didn't know why
the snake didn't choke, the rabbit never
moved, how the jaws kept opening

wider, sucking it down, just so
I am taking this in, slowly,
taking it into my body:

this grief. How slow
the body is to realize.
You are never coming back.

Cate Marvin

Before I go let me thank the man who mugs you,
taking your last paycheck, thank the boss who steals
your tips, thank the women who may break you.

I thank the pens that run out on you midsentence,
the flame that singes your hair, the ticket you can't
use because it's torn. Let me thank the stars

that remind you the eyes that were stars are now
holes. Let me thank the lake that drowns you, the sun
that makes your face old. And thank the street your car

dies in. And thank the brother you find unconscious
with bloody arms, thank the needle that assists in
doing him in—so much a part of you. No thanks

to the skin forgetting the hands it welcomed, your
hands refusing to recall what they happened upon.
How blessed is the body you move in—how gone.

Carol Ann Duffy

Not a red rose or a satin heart.

I give you an onion.
It is a moon wrapped in brown paper.
It promises light
like the careful undressing of love.

Here.
It will blind you with tears
like a lover.
It will make your reflection
a wobbling photo of grief.

I am trying to be truthful.

Not a cute card or a kissogram.

I give you an onion.
Its fierce kiss will stay on your lips,
possessive and faithful
as we are,
for as long as we are.

. . .

Take it.
Its platinum loops shrink to a wedding-ring,
if you like.
Lethal.
Its scent will cling to your fingers,
cling to your knife.

Li-Young Lee

FROM BLOSSOMS | 079

From blossoms comes
this brown paper bag of peaches
we bought from the boy
at the bend in the road where we turned toward
signs painted *Peaches*.

From laden boughs, from hands,
from sweet fellowship in the bins,
comes nectar at the roadside, succulent
peaches we devour, dusty skin and all,
comes the familiar dust of summer, dust we eat.

O, to take what we love inside,
to carry within us an orchard, to eat
not only the skin, but the shade,
not only the sugar, but the days, to hold
the fruit in our hands, adore it, then bite into
the round jubilance of peach.

There are days we live
as if death were nowhere
in the background; from joy
to joy to joy, from wing to wing,
from blossom to blossom to
impossible blossom, to sweet impossible blossom.

William Matthews

ONIONS | 080

How easily happiness begins by
dicing onions. A lump of sweet butter
slithers and swirls across the floor
of the sauté pan, especially if its
errant path crosses a tiny slick
of olive oil. Then a tumble of onions.

This could mean soup or risotto
or chutney (from the Sanskrit
chatni, to lick). Slowly the onions
go limp and then nacreous
and then what cookbooks call clear,
though if they were eyes you could see

clearly the cataracts in them.
It's true it can make you weep
to peel them, to unfurl and to tease
from the taut ball first the brittle,
caramel-colored and decrepit
papery outside layer, the least

recent the reticent onion
wrapped around its growing body,
for there's nothing to an onion
but skin, and it's true you can go on

weeping as you go on in, through
the moist middle skins, the sweetest

and thickest, and you can go on
in to the core, to the bud-like,
acrid, fibrous skins densely
clustered there, stalky and in-
complete, and these are the most
pungent, like the nuggets of nightmare

and rage and murmury animal
comfort that infant humans secrete.
This is the best domestic perfume.
You sit down to eat with a rumor
of onions still on your twice-washed
hands and lift to your mouth a hint

of a story about loam and usual
endurance. It's there when you clean up
and rinse the wine glasses and make
a joke, and you leave the minutest
whiff of it on the light switch,
later, when you climb the stairs.

James Cummins

Reading Hemingway makes me so hungry,
for *jambon*, cheeses, and a dry white wine.
Cold, of course, very cold. And very dry.

Reading Hemingway makes some folks angry:
the hip drinking, the bitter pantomime.
But reading Hemingway makes me hungry

for the good life, the sun, the fish, the sky:
blue air, *white water*, dinner on the line . . .
Had it down cold, he did. And dry. Real dry.

But Papa had it all, the *brio*, the *Brie*:
clear-eyed, tight-lipped, advancing on a *stein* . . .
Reading Hemingway makes me so hungry,

I'd knock down Monsieur Stevens, too, if I
drank too much *retsina* before we dined.
(Too old, that man, and way too cold. And dry

enough to rub one's famished nerves awry,
kept talking past the kitchen's closing time!)
Reading Hemingway makes me so hungry . . .
And cold, of course. So cold. And very dry.

Gerald Stern

I'm eating breakfast even if it means standing
in front of the sink and tearing at the grapefruit,
even if I'm leaning over to keep the juices
away from my chest and stomach and even if a spider
is hanging from my ear and a wild flea
is crawling down my leg. My window is wavy
and dirty. There is a wavy tree outside
with pitiful leaves in front of the rusty fence
and there is a patch of useless rhubarb, the leaves
bent over, the stalks too large and bitter for eating,
and there is some lettuce and spinach too old for picking
beside the rhubarb. This is the way the saints
ate, only they dug for thistles, the feel
of thorns in the throat it was a blessing, my pity
it knows no bounds. There is a thin tomato plant
inside a rolled-up piece of wire, the worms
are already there, the birds are bored. In time
I'll stand beside the rolled-up fence with tears
of gratitude in my eyes. I'll hold a puny
pinched tomato in my open hand,
I'll hold it to my lips. Blessed art Thou,
King of tomatoes, King of grapefruit. The thistle
must have juices, there must be a trick. I hate
to say it but I'm thinking if there is a saint
in our time what will he be, and what will he eat?

I hated rhubarb, all that stringy sweetness—
a fake applesauce—I hated spinach,
always with egg and vinegar, I hated
oranges when they were quartered, that was the signal
for castor oil—aside from the peeled navel
I love the Florida cut in two. I bend
my head forward, my chin is in the air,
I hold my right hand off to the side, the pinkie
is waving; I am back again at the sink;
oh loneliness, I stand at the sink, my garden
is dry and blooming. I love my lettuce, I love
my cornflowers, the sun is doing it all,
the sun and a little dirt and a little water.
I lie on the ground out there, there is one yard
between the house and the tree; I am more calm there
looking back at this window, looking up
a little at the sky, a blue passageway
with smears of white—and grey—a bird crossing
from berm to berm, from ditch to ditch, another one,
a wild highway, a wild skyway, a flock
of little ones to make me feel gay, they fly
down the thruway, I move my eyes back and forth
to see them appear and disappear, I stretch
my neck, a kind of exercise. Ah sky,
my breakfast is over, my lunch is over, the wind

has stopped, it is the hour of deepest thought.
Now I brood, I grimace, how quickly the day goes,
how full it is of sunshine, and wind, how many
smells there are, how gorgeous is the distant
sound of dogs, and engines—Blessed art Thou,
Lord of the falling leaf, Lord of the rhubarb,
Lord of the roving cat, Lord of the cloud.
Blessed art Thou oh grapefruit King of the universe,
Blessed art Thou my sink, oh Blessed art Thou
Thou milkweed Queen of the sky, burster of seeds,
Who bringeth forth juice from the earth.

Joey Roth

I found a small version
Of Yukio Mishima,
On a plate.

He ordered a glass of orange juice
But when he tried to drink
He fell in.

His tiny body was mummified
By the citric acid
Which was a kinder death than his suicide.

He was alive for just a moment while in the glass
And he said something vague
About Japanese nationalism.

Paul Suntup

The toast would taste better with egg, but there aren't any,
so I pour a thimble-sized serving of olive oil on, to make it more

flavorful. I like the taste of olive oil. It reminds me of the time
when I was eighteen and jumped clear over the hood of my car

because I could. To be more specific, olive oil is the part where
I leave the ground and I'm in the air, halfway across. Right then,

before landing on the other side. That's the taste of olive oil.
It also tastes the way Madagascar sounds when you say it

backwards. If there were olive oil cologne, I would wear it and if
there were olive oil goldfish, I would have two in a bowl on the

table. For some reason, it is also a man swallowing lighter
fluid because the pain in his belly is bigger than the Kalahari

Desert. But maybe that's only when you drink it straight; and
sometimes it tastes like Brigitte Bardot. To be more specific,

in the scene where she is sunning naked in Capri, an impossibly
blue ocean wrestling with the sky in the distance.

Debora Greger

And so to the fifteenth century, in a far corner
of the Louvre. Where, when Madonna and Child

stopped to rest on the flight into Egypt,
they found themselves in the Netherlands.

How languid they were, as if too wellborn
to require bones. But two angels were needed

to lift the Virgin's blue train above the Dutch dirt.
And yet a fisherman noticed nothing

but the lack of fish in a greenish lake.
Had the donkey refusing to move

seen something besides the swan gliding away
from *le Maître aux Cygnes* (as the painter,

whose name has been lost, is known)?
In vain the beast's owner held up a cudgel

to the blue velvet of heaven. Would he be struck
by one of the thin gold rays that fell from on high

• • •

indiscriminately? Something had stunted the trees,
over which even the Child towered.

There was no shade to be had, or need of it.
Nothing cast a shadow yet in Western art.

Susan Browne

I'm at a day-long meditation retreat, eight hours of watching
    my mind with my mind,
and I already fell asleep twice and nearly fell out of my chair,
    and it's not even noon yet.

In the morning session, I learned to count my thoughts, ten in
    one minute, and the longest
was to leave and go to San Anselmo and shop, then find an
    outdoor cafe and order a glass

of Sancerre, smoked trout with roasted potatoes and baby
    carrots and a bowl of gazpacho.
But I stayed and learned to name my thoughts; so far they are:
    wanting, wanting, wanting,

wanting, wanting, wanting, wanting, wanting, judgment,
    sadness. *Don't identify with your*
thoughts, the teacher says, *you are not your personality, not your*
    ego-identification,

then he bangs the gong for lunch. Whoever, whatever I am is
    given instruction
in the walking meditation and the eating meditation and walks
    outside with the other

• • •

meditators, and we wobble across the lawn like *The Night of the Living Dead*.
I meditate slowly, falling over a few times because I kept my foot in the air too long,

towards a bench, sit slowly down, and slowly eat my sandwich, noticing the bread,
(sourdough), noticing the taste, (tuna, sourdough), noticing the smell, (sourdough, tuna),

thanking the sourdough, the tuna, the ocean, the boat, the fisherman, the field, the grain,
the farmer, the Saran Wrap that kept this food fresh for this body made of food and desire

and the hope of getting through the rest of this day without dying of boredom.
Sun then cloud then sun. I notice a maple leaf on my sandwich. It seems awfully large.

Slowly brushing it away, I feel so sad I can hardly stand it, so I name my thoughts; they are:
sadness about my mother, judgment about my father, wanting the child I never had.

• • •

I notice I've been chasing the same thoughts like dogs around
the same park most of my life,
notice the leaf tumbling gold to the grass. The gong sounds,
and back in the hall,

I decide to try lying down meditation, and let myself sleep. The
Buddha in my dream is me,
surrounded by dogs wagging their tails, licking my hands.
I wake up

for the forgiveness meditation, the teacher saying, *never put
anyone out of your heart,*
and the heart opens and knows it won't last and will have to
open again and again,

chasing those dogs around and around in the sun then cloud
then sun.

Vijay Seshadri

Near the end of one of the old poems, the son of righteousness,
the source of virtue and civility,
on whose back the kingdom is carried
as on the back of the tortoise the earth is carried,
passes into the next world.
The wood is dark. The wood is dark,
and on the other side of the wood the sea is shallow, warm,
    endless.
In and around it, there is no threat of life—
so little is the atmosphere charged with possibility that
he might as well be wading through a flooded basement.
He wades for what seems like forever,
and never stops to rest in the shade of the metal rain trees
springing out of the water at fixed intervals.
Time, though endless, is also short,
so he wades on, until he walks out of the sea and into the
    mountains,
where he burns on the windward slopes and freezes in the
    valleys.
After unendurable struggles,
he finally arrives at the celestial realm.
The god waits there for him. The god invites him to enter.
But, looking through the glowing portal,
he sees on that happy plain not those he thinks wait eagerly for
    him—

his beloved, his brothers, his companions in war and exile,
all long since dead and gone—
but, sitting pretty and enjoying the gorgeous sunset,
his cousin and bitter enemy, the cause of that war, that exile,
whose arrogance and vicious indolence
plunged the world into grief.
The god informs him that, yes, those he loved have been
      carried down
the river of fire. Their thirst for justice
offended the cosmic powers, who are jealous of justice.
In their place in the celestial realm, called Alaukika in the
      ancient texts,
the breaker of faith is now glorified.
He, at least, acted in keeping with his nature.
Who has not felt a little of the despair the son of righteousness
      now feels,
staring wildly around him?
The god watches, not without compassion and a certain
      wonder.
This is the final illusion,
the one to which all the others lead.
He has to pierce through it himself, without divine assistance.
He will take a long time about it,
with only his dog to keep him company,
the mongrel dog, celebrated down the millennia,

who has waded with him,

shivered and burned with him,

and never abandoned him to his loneliness.

That dog bears a slight resemblance to my dog,

a skinny, restless, needy, overprotective mutt,

who was rescued from a crack house by Suzanne.

On weekends, and when I can shake free during the week,

I take her to the Long Meadow, in Prospect Park, where dogs

are allowed off the leash in the early morning.

She's gray-muzzled and old now, but you can't tell that by the

    way she runs.

David Graham

How shall I not love them, snoozing
right through the Annunciation? They inhabit
the outskirts of every importance, sprawl
dead center in each oblivious household.

They're digging at fleas or snapping at scraps,
dozing with noble abandon while a boy
bells their tails. Often they present their rumps
in the foreground of some martyrdom.

What Christ could lean so unconcernedly
against a table leg, the feast above continuing?
Could the Virgin in her joy match this grace
as a hound sagely ponders an upturned turtle?

No scholar at his huge book will capture
my eye so well as the skinny haunches,
the frazzled tails and serene optimism
of the least of these mutts, curled

in the corners of the world's dazzlement.

Rachel Hadas

One is the color of graham crackers and milk;
cornbread with butter and honey;
a stack of pancakes drenched with maple syrup;
peaches and cream (is anybody hungry?).
The other's tiger markings, gray and white,
are lit like alabaster from within,
foxy, rosy, ruddy; dusky blush.
Who would have thought we were so famished for
the tawny, the caressable? No longer
now splayed out along the floor for coolness,
they reconfigure for the coming season
into shapes of meatloaf, tugboat, owl.

Mark Doty

They lie in parallel rows,
on ice, head to tail,
each a foot of luminosity

barred with black bands,
which divide the scales'
radiant sections

like seams of lead
in a Tiffany window.
Iridescent, watery

prismatics: think abalone,
the wildly rainbowed
mirror of a soapbubble sphere,

think sun on gasoline.
Splendor, and splendor,
and not a one in any way

distinguished from the other
—nothing about them
of individuality. Instead

• • •

they're *all* exact expressions
of the one soul,
each a perfect fulfillment

of heaven's template,
mackerel essence. As if,
after a lifetime arriving

at this enameling, the jeweler's
made uncountable examples,
each as intricate

in its oily fabulation
as the one before.
Suppose we could iridesce,

like these, and lose ourselves
entirely in the universe
of shimmer—would you want

to be yourself only,
unduplicatable, doomed
to be lost? They'd prefer,

. . .

plainly, to be flashing participants,
multitudinous. Even now
they seem to be bolting

forward, heedless of stasis.
They don't care they're dead
and nearly frozen,

just as, presumably,
they didn't care that they were living:
all, all for all,

the rainbowed school
and its acres of brilliant classrooms,
in which no verb is singular,

or every one is. How happy they seem,
even on ice, to be together, selfless,
which is the price of gleaming.

Diane Wald

THE CORGIS OF QUEEN
ELIZABETH | 091

on wednesday september 10th 2003 i was visiting my friend
    larry
who is chronically ill
larry knows everything about the corgis
and queen elizabeth
who now has five or six corgis
who mill about her feet and the feet of her dressmakers
and all the kings and queens before elizabeth
and he knows what the corgis have for breakfast
and he knows that they get fresh vegetables not raw
and they get turkey
in little silver bowls
cut up in little cubes not slices
and queen elizabeth serves them their meals herself
she had a favorite corgi named daisy
whom she buried somewhere on the palace grounds
with a little corgi funeral
and i do not mean to make fun of that
because i am happy she loved her corgi
but let's be clear it does not always mean
that a person who loves a different kind of creature
is totally good
as i understand hitler loved canaries
and not to compare her to hitler

but queen elizabeth also indulges in hunting
and we all know about those presidential dogs

while larry is talking i'm thinking this is very fascinating
but i'm also watching the digital clock
over his shoulder
which displays hours minutes weather wind velocity
and alerts you whenever the airport closes in boston
if there are disasters of any kind
this is a very special clock
that he bought with part of the money that he received
from his suit against the massachusetts bay transit authority
occasioned by a trolley driver closing the door of the trolley
on his already painful foot
as part of his affliction is a dreadful neuropathy
to which he rarely refers
although that trolley incident really pissed him off
because the driver could have easily seen his crutches

he tells me the corgis have their own bedroom
next to the bedroom of queen elizabeth and prince philip
yes the queen does sleep with the prince even now
except on the nights when he's out very late
and comes home after she has retired
when politely he goes and sleeps on a special princely bed

right in his dressing room
the corgis however always sleep in their own room
just next to the queen's own queenly bedroom
and recently when a man
was somehow able to break into the palace
and walk boldly into the queen's suite of rooms
finding the queen cloaked and crowned in terrycloth
as she had just taken her queenly evening bath
and was carrying her gin tray and a big yellow towel
the queen was most relieved that the corgis were not able
to get out of their bedroom
because she feared that they would have used
their little diamond-sharp teeth
to shred the silly man like turkey
so loyal and so fierce (but so sweet) are those corgis

and while larry is telling me about the queen and the corgis
and throwing in a lot of extra information about prince charles
and camilla and how camilla and her father
actually have suites of rooms in one of the royal buildings
where diana's sons now live
i cannot understand how this can be true
but larry swears it is
in any case all this amazing information pours out of larry
in a way that i never would have believed possible

since he is normally a rather circumspect fellow
and while i'm watching the airport clock
over his right shoulder
i'm watching over his left shoulder
his tiny television
which for some unknown reason he has set to show captions
for the hard of hearing
they are showing newly released tapes from al qaeda
showing pictures of osama bin laden
or someone made up to look like osama bin laden
walking up and down the hillsides
somewhere
looking a lot like a shepherd
from the old testament
and underneath the captions are reading
"is it osama?
is it not osama?"
there is an investigation to try to find out
whether the tape is real or a hoax
and whether the soundtrack (or what shows on larry's tv
as italicized captions) was added to the tape after the video
was shot and i'm thinking
what difference does that make
it doesn't mean that it isn't really osama

or even that it isn't really
a shepherd from the old testament

and perhaps it's all happening in cleveland or barcelona or
     honolulu
and not in afghanistan or iraq or hollywood
or any of the places we're always being conditioned to think
are the only places anything of significance ever happens
when really everything is happening right here
right here with the corgis and queen elizabeth and larry
and the trolley driver and the lawyer who handled larry's case
and the democratic presidential candidates
and the people who are sitting out on their stoops
just the way people did fifty years ago
on washington street in jamaica plain
but it's right here and not twenty years ago or five years from
     now and

everything's happening right here
right here where you hear or read this and make up your mind
     about it
right here and right now and not anywhere else forever

May Sarton

They come like deer
To a salt lick,
They come without fear,
Come from far and near
To lick and lick.

The salt, a mystery,
The written word,
Not me.

But the deer, you see,
Are confused.
I, not the word, am used
To fill their need
Like salt or bread.

On some cold winter day
I shall be licked away
Through no deer's fault,
There will be no more salt.

Aimee Nezhukumatathil

AANABHRANDHANMAR MEANS
"MAD ABOUT ELEPHANTS" | 093

Forget trying to pronounce it. What matters
is that in southern India, thousands are afflicted.
And who wouldn't be? Children play with them
in courtyards, slap their gray skin with cupfuls
of water, shoo flies with paper pompoms.
When the head of the household leaves

for business, his elephant weeps fat tears
of joy when he returns. Their baths of husk
and stone last four hours, every wrinkle
rubbed and patted with cinnamon oil.
At festival, silk caps and gold tassels drape
their broad heads. Brides still wear

rings of its stiff tail hair, part of their dowry
to avoid evil eye. A man with blue sandals
told me that elephants are cousins to the clouds—
that they belonged to Lord Indra, king
of the gods, that elephants were his carriage
in the wind—that they once had wings.

Robert Minhinnick

He scans the frames but doesn't stop,
this fox who has come to the museum today,
his eye in the renaissance
and his brush in the baroque.

Between dynasties his footprints
have still to fade, between the Shan and the Yung,
the porcelain atoms shivering at his touch,
ah, lighter than the emperor's breath, drinking rice wine
    from the bowl,
daintier than the eunuch pouring wine.

I came as quickly as I could
but already the fox had left the Industrial Revolution
    behind,
his eye has swept the age of atoms,
the Taj Mahal within the molecule.

The fox is in the folios and the fossils, I cry.
The fox is in photography and the folk studies department.
The fox is in the flux of the foyer,
the fox is in the flock.
The fox is in the flock.

. . .

Now the fox sniffs at the dodo
and at the door of Celtic orthography.
The grave-goods, the chariots, the gods of darkness,
he has made their acquaintance on previous occasions.

There, beneath the leatherbacked turtle he goes,
the turtle black as an oildrum,
under the skeleton of the whale he skedaddles,
the whalebone silver as bubblewrap.

Through the light of Provence moves the fox, through
the Ordovician era and the Sumerian summer,
greyblue the brush on him, this one who has seen so much,
blood on the bristles of his mouth,
and on his suit of iron filings the air fans like silk.

Through the cubists and the surrealists
This fox shimmies surreptitiously,
past the artist who has sawn himself in half
under the formaldehyde sky
goes this fox shiny as a silver
fax in his fox coat,
for at a fox trot travels this fox
backwards and forwards in the museum.

• • •

Under the bells of brugmansia
that lull the Ecuadoran botanists to sleep,
over the grey moss of Iceland
further and further goes this fox,
passing the lambs at the feet of Jesus,
through the tear in Dante's cloak.

How long have I legged it
after his legerdemain, this fox
in the labyrinth, this fox that never hurries
yet passes an age in a footfall, this fox
from the forest of the portrait gallery
to engineering's cornfield sigh?

I will tell you this.
He is something to follow,
this red fellow.
This fox I foster—
he is the future.
No-one else
has seen him yet.
But they are closing
the iron doors.

Laurie Lamon

PRAISE | 095

I heard the dogs before
I opened the door late, after work—
first Maude who was dancing
in praise of my arrival for all she knew
it was: presence without end,
the end of waiting, the end
of boredom—
    and then Li Po,
who, in the middle of his life,
learning to make his feelings known
as one who has carried breath
and heart close to the earth seven
times seven years, in praise
of silence and loneliness, climbed
howling, howling from his bed.

Reader, you have seen them: they have inched past you
    at the poetry reading, the concert, the play, their "Sorry!"
        yet another way of saying "Move your damn knees, bud!"
And there are the girlfriends and wives, just behind,
    smiling and shrugging as if to say, "That's Bob for ya!"

Harry here successfully reversed a long-standing precedent
    in court today; why can't he bear Rossini's Quartet in
        D Major?
        And Pete, making his way down row K, stopped a mitral
        valve
from fibrillating and saved a boy's life, but he can't make it through
    act two of Turgenev's *A Month in the Country*?

I know—they think the actors and musicians will make them gay.
    Don't they know there's an unwritten showbiz rule
        which says gays can kiss once on stage but not twice
because that means they like it?
    Besides, one will never be bored as long as one pays
        attention,

even if few playgoers will be as attentive as John Wilkes Booth was,
    who knew that the line that drew the loudest burst of laughter
        in *An American Cousin* was when one character said to
        another

"Well, I guess I know enough to turn you inside out,
        you sockdologising old man-trap,"

whereupon he fired his fatal shot, the noise of the pistol
            muffled by the audience's guffaws, and made his escape.
                On nonfatal nights at the theater, there are many *comic*
                moments,
such as those provided by one Robert Coates,
            arguably the worst actor ever to tread the boards,

whose Romeo dusted the floor with a handkerchief
            and set his hat on a pillow before he took the fatal
                    poison,
                whose backward leap would have made any member
of the Purdue diving team proud, and who, when a spectator
        shouted
            "Die again, Romeo!" took another swig and died a second
            time.

Even when high culture is dull, it's never dumb,
            like soap operas, where there's a knock on the door,
                and the person running to open it cries out,
"Oh, Gary, thank God you're here!
        I'm pregnant, and Frank doesn't know about us,

• • •

so he thinks the baby is his, and—oh, hello, Frank . . . ,"
    and where the shows are so cheaply produced that
        retakes
      are impossible, so that, on a soap I watched once,
a guy playing a doctor gets up and hits his knee
      so hard against his desk that he goes "Gnnngghhh!"

but continues the scene anyway, though wincing so hard
      it's impossible not to cringe yourself
        as he tells his patient "There may not—holy Christ!—
be anything major wrong—goddammit . . . ,"
      and if this is true, which it is, how equally true is it that

high culture is not governed by such elitists as the Italian
    melomani
      or "music lovers" who fuss over such popular acts
      as the Three Tenors and who "are right," says the
        singer
Alessandro Safina, although "there are so few of them, really,"
    that it makes no difference whether they are right or not.

The other night at the poetry reading, a kid in a baseball cap
    got up
      in the middle of a poem and tapped his girlfriend
        on the head with his car keys. That girl was pissed—

one extra-credit opportunity down the drain there!—
　　　but she followed him out into the parking lot anyway.

Women, it might be up to you. Women,
　　　when your fellow hands you your purse or taps you
　　　　　on the head with his car keys or pushes off from his seat
and says he "can't stand any more of this shit,"
　　　you might have to be the one who sputters "Richard, sit
　　　　　down!"

It might be you who, while caressing his thigh in a way
　　　that suggests that the full cafeteria of sensory delights
　　　　　will be open to him all night long
if only he'll sit through the denouement,
　　　the final strophe, the ultimate *allegro ma non troppo*,

it might be you who grabs him by the *coglioni* and hisses,
　　　as Charles Ives did when some idiot booed
　　　　　a 1931 performance of his work,
"Stop being such a goddamned sissy! Why can't you stand up
　　　before fine strong music like this and use your ears like a
　　　　　man?"

Your guy will be startled! He may even begin to whimper, his
　　　great head

sagging to your shoulder, where he sobs his heart out,
crying "The bad men hurt me, Mommy—
the bad men hurt me!" And you'll caress him, you'll say "There,
there, darling,
we'll go home soon. We'll have a snack."

Carl Dennis

AMNESTY | 097

This will inform those who've borrowed
Items of portable property in the last twelve years
From Mr. Harvey Krugman, of 11 Herkimer Street,
And never returned them that all month long
They won't have to knock at his door
And explain their delinquency to be forgiven.
They're hereby invited to come at night, unseen,
And leave the items in back, in the boxes provided,
Items replaced long ago, to be sure, but not forgotten,
Though he's forgotten the parties he's loaned them to.

Are his edgers or clippers now hanging in your garage?
Is his seed spreader there, leaf blower, or mulcher?
Is there a hook in your kitchen where his pancake griddle
Hangs within easy reach, or a dining-room cabinet
That displays, through its leaded glass, his punch bowl?
It isn't attachment to things that's the issue here
But Mr. Krugman's faith, almost expired now,
In human pledges and promises. Won't you help revive it
By a quick return of the items in question,
Proving your fault has never been crass indifference
To common courtesy, but simple forgetfulness?

• • •

Don't be embarrassed if the item's in bad condition.
He'd be happy if you returned the book you borrowed
Five years ago, now out of print,
However blackened it is by basement mildew.
And don't assume he's foolish to have been so trusting.
His loans don't spring from an all-too rosy
Assessment of the world he lives in
But from the first commandment in his private decalogue:
Act, now and then, as if the world wished for
Were here already. After that, he figures, it's up to the world
To decide if any improvement is possible.

So take the time this weekend to examine
Your shelves, closets, and cabinets with the question
How each particular item happened to come there.
For those you believe to be gifts, try to recall
The names of the givers, or the occasion,
Or at least your feelings when you first enjoyed them.
If you've forgotten, maybe Mr. Krugman,
If you're willing to knock at his door
And show the item, can jog your memory.

. . .

Then he may show you the serving plate
Left long ago by an unknown guest
And never reclaimed. Beautiful cut glass
That he's kept safe in a drawer, unused,
To dream of the place where it was cherished.
If it looks like yours, you can take it home.

George Green

STEPHEN DUCK AND
EDWARD CHICKEN | 098

failed to make it into Schmidt's *Lives of the Poets.*
Duck, "The Thresher Poet of Pewsey Downs,"
would vault into the court of Caroline
and marry Sarah Big, her housekeeper.
"The Muse's Darling, Reverend Duck is dead,"
wrote Mary Collier, "The Poetical Washer-Woman,"
upon the unhappy event.
Also lamenting Duck were Henry Jones,
"The Poetical Bricklayer," and "Lactilla,
The Poetical Milkmaid of Clifton Hill."
Lactilla later wrote *The Royal Captives,*
an elephantine novel in five volumes,
which kept the wistful milkmaid at her desk
like a galley slave chained drooping to an oar.

I'd like to tell you more but Southey's splendid
Lives of the Uneducated Poets
is unavailable today from Bobst Library.
He made his pile off Valium, Elmer Bobst,
and that's just fine with me.
A Valium might have rescued Reverend Duck,
who drowned himself, Lord help us,
in a pond behind a rowdy, rustic tavern.
And while we're at it, pass the Valium, please,

to John Gould Fletcher (decades out of print),
who won the Pulitzer in '39,
drowned himself in a murky Ozark duck pond,
and failed, likewise, to make it into Schmidt.
He was rich, I think. Chicken was maybe a curate.

"The Poetical Bag-lady of Astor Place"
boards the 6 train and curses the entire car
for being "illiterate." "Spell mayonnaise,"
she hollers in my face. "Spell mayonnaise!"
And, discombobulated, I cannot.

Christina Daub

Ice swan, *artiste*,
gilder of essays,
king of bibliographies,
there he is by the bookshelf
spouting aphorisms,
Ibid perched like a parrot,
chatting now
in Proust's mottled shadow
or aping Yeats,
Ibid, *flateur*,
quoting the In crowd,
Ibid by the punch bowl
with a ladle of quips,
he gives a toast,
signs a book
with someone else's name,
wants only an Ibid of his own:
Ibid: little brother
who won't be left home.

C. K. Williams

He's not sure how to get the jack on—he must have recently
    bought the car, although it's an ancient,
impossibly decrepit, barely holding-together Chevy: he has to
    figure out how each part works,
the base plate, the pillar, the thing that hooks to the bumper,
    even the four-armed wrench,
before he can get it all together, knock the hubcap off and
    wrestle free the partly rusted nuts.
This all happens on a bed of sheet ice: it's five below, the
    coldest January in a century.
Cars slip and skid a yard away from him, the flimsy jack is
    desperately, precariously balanced,
and meanwhile, when he goes into the trunk to get the spare, a
    page of old newspaper catches his attention
and he pauses, rubbing his hands together, shoulders hunched,
    for a full half minute, reading.

Louis Simpson

Dickinson had a cockatoo
she called Sémiramis
and loved dearly.

Whitman was a trencherman,
his favorite dish
a mulligan stew.

Frost went for long walks,
Eliot played croquet,
Pound took fencing lessons.

There is a snapshot of Yeats
in a garden with a woman
naked to the waist and smiling.

Auden when he was old
counted the sheets of toilet paper
that a visitor used.

Julianna Baggott

BLURBS | 102

I don't want to be *a national treasure*,
too old-codgery, something wheeled out
of a closet to cut ribbon. I prefer
resident genius, or for the genius
to be at least *undeniable*.
I'd like to steer away from the declaration
by far her best. Too easily I read,
the predecessors were weary immigrant stock.
The same goes for *working at the height
of her powers*, as if it's obvious
I'm teetering on the edge of senility.
I don't want to have to look things up:
lapidary style? I'd prefer not to be *a talent*;
as if my mother has dressed me
in a spangled leotard, tap shoes,
my hair in Bo-Peep pin curls.
But I like *sexy*, even if unearned.
I like *elegance*, *bite*. I want someone
to confess they've fallen in love with me
and another to say, *No, she's mine.*
And a third to just come out with it:
she will go directly to heaven.

Adam Zagajewski

Those were the long afternoons when poetry left me.
The river flowed patiently, nudging lazy boats to sea.
Long afternoons, the coast of ivory.
Shadows lounged in the streets, haughty manikins in
    shopfronts
stared at me with bold and hostile eyes.

Professors left their schools with vacant faces,
as if the *Iliad* had finally done them in.
Evening papers brought disturbing news,
but nothing happened, no one hurried.
There was no one in the windows, you weren't there;
even nuns seemed ashamed of their lives.

Those were the long afternoons when poetry vanished
and I was left with the city's opaque demon,
like a poor traveler stranded outside the Gare du Nord
with his bulging suitcase wrapped in twine
and September's black rain falling.

Oh, tell me how to cure myself of irony, the gaze
that sees but doesn't penetrate; tell me how to cure myself
of silence.

Translated by Clare Cavanagh

R. S. Gwynn

SHAKESPEAREAN SONNET | 104

(With a first line taken from the tv listings)

A man is haunted by his father's ghost.
A boy and girl love while their families fight.
A Scottish king is murdered by his host.
Two couples get lost on a summer night.
A hunchback murders all who block his way.
A ruler's rivals plot against his life.
A fat man and a prince make rebels pay.
A noble Moor has doubts about his wife.
An English king decides to conquer France.
A duke learns that his best friend is a she.
A forest sets the scene for this romance.
An old man and his daughters disagree.
A Roman leader makes a big mistake.
A sexy queen is bitten by a snake.

Jack Myers

I can feel my ship about to come in.
A white ship in a snowstorm
moving in.

The ship is made of gulls
huddled together
in the shape of a ship.

When it arrives, they will fly out into the storm,
leaving a space inside it
clear as reason.

I can tell there's going to be a blizzard
of being somewhere else
any minute

because of time's noise eating itself up
that is the noise of listening
that looks like a seething, florid whiteout of wings.

James Tate

An ad in the newspaper said that a local author
would be signing his new book at the bookstore today.
I didn't even know we had any local authors. I was
going to be downtown anyway, so I decided to drop in
and see what he looked like. He was short and fat
and ugly, but all kinds of beautiful women were flirting
with him and laughing at every little joke he made.
Even though I didn't know anything about his book, I
wished I had written it. A man came up to me and said,
"I hated it when the little girl died. I just couldn't
stop crying." "Thank God for the duck," I said. He
took a step back from me. "I don't remember the duck,"
he said. "Well, then, I'm afraid you missed the whole
point of the book. The duck is absolutely central,
it's the veritable linchpin of the whole denouement,"
I said. (I had learned that word in high school, and
now it served me well.) "But what about the little
girl?" the man asked, with a painful look of bewilder-
ment on his face. "She should have been shot a hundred
pages earlier," I said. "I don't think I like you,"
the man said, and walked away clutching his book.
I looked over at the author. He was signing a young
woman's cleavage, and the other women were laughing
and pulling open their blouses to be signed. I had
never even thought of writing a novel. Now, my mind

was thrashing about. The man I had offended earlier walked up to me and offered me a glass of wine. "If I may ask you, sir, why were you so rude to me?" he said. I looked up from the abyss and said, "Because I am nothing. Because I am a speck of dust floating in infinite darkness. Because you have feelings and you care. Do you understand me now?" "Perfectly," he said. "Cheers!"

Franz Wright

One of the few pleasures of writing
is the thought of one's book in the hands of a kind-hearted
intelligent person somewhere. I can't remember what the
     others are right now.
I just noticed that it is my own private

National I Hate Myself and Want to Die Day
(which means the next day I will love my life
and want to live forever). The forecast calls
for a cold night in Boston all morning

and all afternoon. They say
tomorrow will be just like today,
only different. I'm in the cemetery now
at the edge of town, how did I get *here*?

A sparrow limps past on its little bone crutch saying
I am Federico Garcia Lorca
risen from the dead—
literature will lose, sunlight will win, don't worry.

Paul Durcan

THE POETRY READING LAST NIGHT IN THE ROYAL HIBERNIAN HOTEL | 108

The main thing—the first and last thing—to say
About the poetry reading last night in the Royal Hibernian
　　　Hotel
Is that the Royal Hibernian Hotel does not exist;
It was demolished last year to make way for an office block.
If, therefore, anyone was to ask me what a poetry reading is,
I should have the utmost difficulty in enlightening them,
All the more so after having attended last night's poetry
　　　reading
In the Royal Hibernian Hotel which does not exist.
A poetry reading appears to be a type of esoteric social ritual
Peculiar to the cities of northern Europe and North America.
What happens is that for one reason or another,
Connected usually with moods in adolescence
To do with Family and School and Sexuality,
A chap—or a dame—begins writing things
Which he—she—calls 'Poetry'
And over the years—especially between the ages of fourteen and
　　　sixty-four—
What with one kind of wangling or another,
He—she—publishes seventeen or nineteen slim volumes
Entitled *Stones* or *Bricks* or *Pebbles* or *Gravel;*
Or *History Notes* or *Digs* or *French Class.*

He—she—is hellbent on boring the pants off people
And that's where the poetry-reading trick comes in.
The best poets are the poets who can bore you the most,
Such as the fellow last night who was so adept at boring us
That for the entire hour that he stood there mumbling and
     whining
My mind was altogether elsewhere with the reindeer
In Auden's Cemetery for the Silently and Very Fast.
A poetry reading is a ritual in communal schizophrenia
In which the minds of the audience are altogether elsewhere
While their bodies are kept sitting upright or in position.
Afterwards it is the custom to clap as feebly as you can—
A subtle exercise appropriate to the overall scheme.
To clap feebly—or to feebly clap—is as tricky as it sounds.
It is the custom then to invite the poet to autograph the slim
     volume
And while the queue forms like the queue outside a
     confessional,
The poet cringing archly on an upright chair,
You say to your neighbour 'A fine reading, wasn't it?'
To which he must riposte
'Indeed—nice to see you lying through your teeth.'
The fully clothèd audience departs, leaving the poet

Who bored the pants off them
Laughing all the way to the toilet
Of a hotel that does not exist,
Thence to the carpark that *does* exist
Where he has left his Peugeot with the broken exhaust pipe.
'Night-night'—he mews to the automatic carpark attendant
Who replies with one bright, emphatic, onomatopoeic
    monosyllable:
'Creep.'

Christopher Howell

When Keats, at last beyond the curtain
of love's distraction, lay dying in his room
on the Piazza di Spagna, the melody of the Bernini
Fountain "filling him like flowers,"
he held his breath like a coin, looked out
into the moonlight and thought he saw snow.
He did not suppose it was fever or the body's
weakness turning the mind. He thought, "England!"
and there he was, secretly, for the rest
of his improvidently short life: up to his neck
in sleigh bells and the impossibly English cries
of street vendors, perfect
and affectionate as his soul.
For days the snow and statuary sang him so far
beyond regret that if now you walk rancorless
and alone there, in the piazza, the white shadow
of his last words to Severn, "Don't be frightened,"
may enter you.

Peter Pereira

If you believe in the magic of language,
then *Elvis* really *Lives*
and *Princess Diana* foretold *I end as car spin.*

If you believe the letters themselves
contain a power within them,
then you understand
what makes *outside tedious,*
how *desperation* becomes *a rope ends it.*

The circular logic that allows *senator* to become *treason,*
and *treason* to become *atoners.*

That *eleven plus two* is *twelve plus one,*
and an *admirer* is also *married.*

That if you could just re-arrange things the right way
you'd find your true life,
the right path, the answer to your questions:
you'd understand how *the Titanic*
turns into *that ice tin,*
and *debit card* becomes *bad credit.*

How *listen* is the same as *silent,*
and not one letter separates *stained* from *sainted.*

Charles Bernstein

I warrant that this
poem is entirely my
own work and that
the underlying ideas
concepts, and make-up
of the poem have not
been taken from any
other source or any
other poem but rather
originate with this poem.
I further attest that no
one except me, the author
and party to this binding
agreement, has any title
claim, or proprietary
interest in the poem.

I hereby indemnify
the publisher against
any action that can
be taken against the
poem, warranted or
unwarranted, including
libel, defamation, or
infringement on any

trademark, copyright
or patent, irrespective
of any intention or
lack of intention, state
of mind or aesthetic
philosophy. I further
attest that this poem
has not been previously
published, in part or in
whole, in any print or
electronic form, or in
translation, or performed
as part of a reading
musical, review, lecture
or show.

I grant the publisher
worldwide rights to
the poem, including
serial, periodical,
newspaper, magazine
book, bookazine, poster
indoor and outdoor
display rights, and also
digital, paradigital, and

postdigital rights, as well
as the rights to use the
poem in secondary
publications and markets
including franchise and
commercial applications.

The poem will be
copyrighted in the name
of the publisher and the
author hereby and forthwith
without prejudice or duress
and with full consent
agreement, acquiescence
and concurrence relinquishes
rights to republish the
poem in any form, print or
electronic, or perform
the poem at any fair
show, reading, lecture
musical, or review, without
permission, notarized and
in writing, from the
publisher.

. . .

I agree to furnish the publisher
at my own expense and expeditiously
an electronic copy of the poem
as well as one hard copy or print-out.
I agree to review proofs of the poems
and return them, at my own expense
within 36 hours of their receipt.
The proofs will be delivered any
time from later today until 3 January
2010.

In exchange for granting
the publisher the aforesaid
rights, I will receive, as
payment in full, and as
full recompense against
any claims, levies, fees
honoraria, emoluments
endorsements, rights
permissions, or royalties
domestic or global, printed
or electronic, digital
paradigital, and postdigital—
the opportunity to subscribe
to the publication in which

the poem will first appear
at forty percent discount
from the full subscription
price. To exercise this option
I agree to make payment in
full in the next thirty (3o)
days.

Mark Aiello

I love how books begin; those passages
that lead us by the hand across
the luxurious lawns, that portage us
gently up the gravel drive,
toward the manor house.

The author is still a kind host here,
anxious that we mingle
with the other weekend guests, that we note
how even the banisters are polished for us,
that we feel free to walk out
with the lady of the house and smoke
a cigarette, down the grand alley of elms.

We're not expected to have things down pat
yet, like the family tree, or the route to the old Abbey.
Nothing really happens now,
beyond the delivery of breakfast trays.
It's not scheduled to rain
for two more chapters, and no one
who matters to us has died yet.

David Lehman

DENIAL | 113

I am not hungover.
I am *not* hungover.
Not hungover am I.
Am I hungover? Not!
Hungover am I not.
Am hungover? Not I.
I hungover not am.
I am hungover. (Not).
Not I am hungover.
Hungover I am not.
Am I not hungover?
Not am I hungover.
I not am hungover.
Hungover not am I.

Tom Wayman

Taken from A Checklist to Aid in the Detection of
Learning Disabilities

Loses his position on worksheet or page in textbook
May speak much but makes little sense
Cannot give clear verbal instructions
Does not understand what he reads
Does not understand what he hears
Cannot handle "yes-no" questions

Has great difficulty interpreting proverbs
Has difficulty recalling what he ate for breakfast, etc.
Cannot tell a story from a picture
Cannot recognize visual absurdities

Has difficulty classifying and categorizing objects
Has difficulty retaining such things as
addition and subtraction facts, or multiplication tables
May recognize a word one day and not the next

John Ashbery

What is written on the paper
on the table by the bed? Is there something there
or was that from another last night?

Why is that bird ignoring us,
pausing in mid-flight, to take another direction?
Is it feelings of guilt about the spool
it dropped on the bank of a stream,
into which it eventually rolled? Dark spool,
moving oceanward now—what other fate could have been
    yours?
You could have lived in a drawer
for many years, imprisoned, a ward of the state. Now you are
    free
to call the shots pretty much as they come.
Poor, bald thing.

Naomi Shihab Nye

The river is famous to the fish.

The loud voice is famous to the silence,
which knew it would inherit the earth
before anybody said so.

The cat sleeping on the fence is famous to the birds
watching him from the birdhouse.

The tear is famous, briefly, to the cheek.

The idea you carry close to your bosom
is famous to your bosom.

The boot is famous to the earth,
more famous than the dress shoe,
which is famous only to floors.

The bent photograph is famous to the one who carries it,
and not at all famous to the one who is pictured.

I want to be famous to shuffling men,
who smile while crossing streets,
sticky children in grocery lines,
famous as the one who smiled back.

• • •

I want to be famous in the way a pulley is famous,
or a buttonhole, not because it did anything spectacular,
but because it never forgot what it did.

Stephen Dunn

A doll's pink, broken-off arm
was floating in a pond
a man had come to with his dog.
The arm had no sad child nearby
to say it was hers, no parent to rescue it
with a stick or branch,

and this pleased the man to whom
absence always felt like opportunity.
He imagined a girl furious
at her younger sister, taking it out on her
one limb at a time.

Yet the sun was glancing off
the arm's little pink fingers,
and the pond's heart-shaped lily pads
seemed to accentuate an oddness,
which he thought beautiful.

When he and the dog looked for
the doll's body but couldn't find it,
a different image came to him,
of a father who hated the fact
that his son liked dolls.
What was floating there

was a punishment that didn't work,
for the boy had come to love
his one-armed doll even more.
Once again the man was struck
by how much misery
the human spirit can absorb.

His dog wanted to move on,
enough of this already.
But the man was creating little waves
with his hands, and the arm, this thing
his wife was sure to question,
was slowly bobbing toward him.

Paul Violi

We, the naturally hopeful,
Need a simple sign
For the myriad ways we're capsized.
We, who love precise language,
Need a finer way to convey
Disappointment and perplexity.
For speechlessness and all its inflections,
For up-ended expectations,
For every time we're ambushed
By trivial or stupefying irony,
For pure incredulity, we need
The inverted exclamation point.
For the dropped smile, the limp handshake,
For whoever has just unwrapped a dumb gift,
Or taken the first sip of a flat beer,
Or felt love or pond ice
Give way underfoot, we deserve it.
We need it for the air pocket, the scratch shot,
The child whose ball doesn't bounce back,
The flat tire at journey's outset,
The odyssey that ends up in Weehauken.
But mainly because I need it—here and now
As I sit outside the Caffe Reggio
Staring at my espresso and cannoli

After this middle-aged couple
Came strolling by and he suddenly
Veered and sneezed all over my table
And she said to him, "See, *that's* why
I don't like to eat outside."

Mark Perlberg

The Chinese painters didn't use
a vanishing point to show perspective.
    Washes of light and lighter color
    indicated distances—past cliffs, streams
    and humped bridges, past water falling
    from the lip of a rock into a gorge,
    out to farthest pales and shallows,
    where the Immortals ride great fishes and turtles,
    sporting in the unseen world.

Anthony Hecht

Ground lapis for the sky, and scrolls of gold,
Before which shepherds kneel, gazing aloft
At visiting angels clothed in egg-yolk gowns,
Celestial tinctures smuggled from the East,
From sunlit Eden, the palmed and plotted banks
Of sun-tanned Aden. Brought home in fragile grails,
Planted in England, rising at Eastertide,
Their petals cup stamens of topaz dust,
The powdery stuff of cooks and cosmeticians.
But to the camel's-hair tip of the finest brush
Of Brother Anselm, it is the light of dawn,
Gilding the hems, the sleeves, the fluted pleats
Of the antiphonal archangelic choirs
Singing their melismatic *pax in terram.*
The child lies cribbed below, in bestial dark,
Pale as the tiny tips of crocuses
That will find their way to the light through drifts of snow.

Robert Wrigley

HIGHWAY 12, JUST EAST OF PARADISE, IDAHO | 121

The doe, at a dead run, was dead
the instant the truck hit her.
In the headlights I saw her tongue
extend and her eyes go shocked and vacant.
Launched at a sudden right angle—say
from twenty miles per hour south to fifty
miles per hour east—she skated
many yards on the slightest toe-edge tips
of her dainty deer hooves, then fell
slowly, inside the speed of her new trajectory,
not pole-axed but stunned, away
from me and the truck's decelerating pitch.
She skidded along the right lane's
fog line true as a cue ball,
until her neck caught a sign post
that spun her across both lanes and out of sight
beyond the edge. For which, I admit, I was grateful,
the road there being dark, narrow, and shoulderless,
and home, with its lights, not far away.

Kirsten Kaschock

MAN-MADE | 122

for Mitchell Baker

An airplane is a terrible thing.
It has a terrible height.
Airplanes are moveable Babels, and I
and you, and everyone
know not to reach that way for God, up—
that a god
is a small thing and comes by being quiet.
An airplane is also steel, and steel
is terrible. And Pittsburgh a terrible place
because of the steel. We should
not move there. If we do not move at all,
a god may come by not flying.
Not by wings by quiet
a trembling that begins no war
may work itself from underneath
skin or earth, a warmth
may bloom in the mouth like an alcohol
not at all like alcohol. This is how a god
would begin in you, or anyone,
or me. Not blown
across an ocean or pumped out of depths
slick and flammable. Aren't gods
what happen in us

when we listen for gods?
I do not think a god enlists machines
for proof. And gods do not favor
the way birds move
over the flight of dolphins.
It is a terrible thing
for you to think so.

David Kirby

Friend tells me *her* friend kept an amp
  in the trunk of their car so they could get into shows,
elbowing the doorman aside with an "Excuse me,
    excuse me, damn it!" and no one saying a thing,
because who'd go to all that trouble
  if they weren't part of the entertainment?

As it says on the wall of every dry cleaner's in America,
  there's no substitute for hard work.
A writer might say, as Gide did, "I rewrite in order
    to be reread." Or he might echo
Thomas Mann and say, "A writer is someone for whom writing
  is more difficult than it is for other people."

Or he might open the paper and read "Dagwood": in today's
  episode,
  Mr. Dithers is saying, "Bumstead! Why haven't you
started on that report to the stockholders?!"
    and Dagwood replies, "I'm waiting for inspiration
to strike," but then he's flying through the air,
  and now he's at his computer: "Dear Stockholders. . . ."

And look at him—he doesn't even have a hair
  out of place! Ol' Dag is bowed but he isn't bloody;

he is the buck private of his soul. Later, he will have
  a big sandwich and a long nap while Daisy lies
alongside the sofa adoringly, waiting for him to wake,
  but right now he's got that report to write.

Maybe "Dagwood" should be on the dry cleaner's wall.
  The Hasidim have a tale about a rabbi named Meir
who used to worry that God would reproach him
  in his final days and say, "Meir! Why did you not
become Meir?" Here's a formula for you:
  1 Dagwood + 1 Mr. Dithers = 1 Meir.

Notice it's always "Mr. Dithers," by the way,
  and never "Julius," whereas it's either "Dagwood"
or "Bumstead" and never "Mr. Bumstead."
  But amps—I've never lifted one—are really heavy,
  aren't they?
Didn't Ginger Rogers say she had to do everything
  Fred Astaire did, only backwards and in heels?

Robert Bly

Those great sweeps of snow that stop suddenly six feet from the
    house . . .
Thoughts that go so far.
The boy gets out of high school and reads no more books;
The son stops calling home.
The mother puts down her rolling pin and makes no more
    bread.
And the wife looks at her husband one night at a party, and
    loves him no more.
The energy leaves the wine, and the minister falls leaving the
    church.
It will not come closer—
The one inside moves back, and the hands touch nothing, and
    are safe.

The father grieves for his son, and will not leave the room
    where the coffin stands.
He turns away from his wife, and she sleeps alone.

And the sea lifts and falls all night, the moon goes on through
    the unattached heavens alone.
The toe of the shoe pivots

In the dust . . .

And the man in the black coat turns, and goes back down the
hill.

No one knows why he came, or why he turned away, and did not
climb the hill.

Paul Violi

The mailbox, painted dark blue,
sits atop a tilted cedar post.
It has a little red flag on one side
and it is altogether remarkable.

The Toyota in the driveway
is very old and is said
to have come from Japan.

There is in the hallway
an immense dogfood bowl.
It is made of iridescent pink plastic.
It is, as I have said, immense
and it is hideous.

In the kitchenette is a statuette
of Ceres, Goddess of Wheaties.

The dishwasher is a Kenmore
and altogether worthy of praise.

In the foyer the oversized painting
of a pork chop provides

visitors many opportunities
for conversation.

In the servants' quarters
there are many impressive works
that stress the imminence of death
and the probability of hell fire.

Placed on the broad maplewood table
beside bottles of cognac
there is a recording device
with a silver megaphone
into which natives are often
invited to shout
the oral histories of their people.

We whose hearts have been gripped
by life, scoff at the idea of art
as mere ornamentation: So they
seem to proclaim,
the three statues that adorn
the neighbor's lawn, plaster deer
with real bulletholes in them.

Bruce A. Jacobs

JEEP CHEROKEE | 126

You've never known
a single Indian
who wasn't painted
onto a football helmet
or branded in chrome
on a tailgate,
but there you go,
off mashing the landscape
like some edge-city explorer,
flinging yourself toward
new worlds beyond the driveway,
Lewis and Clark
with a seat belt.
Go ahead, you trampling trooper,
you goose-stepping little
Godzilla, you shining beast
of raging fashion,
riding the big teeth
of your tires as if you
would ever follow a dirt road
anywhere but to a car wash.
This is America,
and you're free to drive
anything you can buy
but I will tell you:

Hitler would love this car—
a machine in which
even the middle class
can master the world,
purchase their way through peril
safely as senators.
This is a car for
a uniformed strongman,
a one-car motorcade
through a thatched village
of strangers.
This is the car that will
replace Prozac.
This is the car that Barbie buys
with mad money
after the date with Angry White Ken.
This is the car every KKK member
wants to drive after dark.
This is the car that makes it safe
to be hateful in public.
Go ahead. Climb in. Look
at yourself, way up there
on the bridge of this
thick-windowed ship of enterprise.
Everybody knows

the only way today is to
buy your way through,
be bigger, be better,
be a bully, be a barger,
be sure you're safe from the poor,
bustle your way through
each day's bombardment
with the muscle of royalty.
You've got the power
to bring back the monarchy
four fat tires at a time.
Go anywhere. You're entitled.
You have squasher's rights.
Onward! Accelerate,
you brawny bruising winner,
you self-saluting junta on wheels,
you reclaimer of gold-bricked streets.
Democracy is for people
stuck in small cars
and God has never ruled
through traffic laws.
Get used to the feeling
of having your way.
Each broad cut of the steering wheel
is your turn at conquest,

the power-assisted triumph
of the me
in heavy traffic.
You are rolling proof
that voting is stupid,
that the whole damn machine is fixed
before it leaves the factory,
that fairness is a showroom,
that togetherness is for bus riders,
that TV has the right idea:
there is just you in a small room
on the safe side of glass,
with desire spread out before you
like a ballroom without walls,
and you will not be denied,
you've got the moves and the view,
you don't need government, unions,
bank regulation, mercy,
the soft hands of strangers.
You've got 4-wheel drive
and a phone, you've got
the friendship of a reinforced chassis,
you've got empathy for dictators
without knowing it,
you've got freedom from rear-view mirrors,

you've got wide-bodied citizenship,
you've gained Custer's Revenge:
caissons packed with children and soccer balls
coasting across the plowed prairie,
history remodeled with one great
blaring of jingles and horns:

Hail Citizen King!
Hail the unswerving settler!
Hail the rule of logo!
Hail Jeep Cherokee!

Kay Ryan

Not every day
is a good day
for the elfin tailor.
Some days
the stolen cloth
reveals what it
was made for:
a handsome weskit
or the jerkin
of an elfin sailor.
Other days
the tailor
sees a jacket
in his mind
and sets about
to find the fabric.
But some days
neither the idea
nor the material
presents itself;
and these are
the hard days
for the tailor elf.

Dick Allen

Something was out there on the lake, just barely
visible in the dark.
I knelt and stared, trying to make it out,
trying to mark

its position relative to mine,
and the picturesque willow, the moon-silvered diving board
on the opposite shore. I listened hard
but heard

no sound from it, although I cupped one ear
as I knelt in the cove,
wondering how far I should take this, if I should seek
someone to row out there with me. Yet it didn't move

or grow darker or lighter. Most shapes,
you know what they are:
a rock-garden serpent, a house in the mist, a man's head,
an evening star,

but not this one. Whatever was out there kept changing
from large to small.
The mass of a wooden coffin surfaced,
then the head of an owl,

• • •

a tree limb, a window, a veil—
I couldn't resolve it. I ran one hand through my hair
as I stood up, shrugging. I had just turned fifty
and whatever it was that might be floating there

I didn't want it to be. Too much before
that came unbidden into my life
I'd let take me over. I knelt again and stared again.
Something was out there just beyond the cove.

Glyn Maxwell

Los Angeles. So just
guess what I saw: not the dust
or the wide jammed road, not that. And not
the park where enormous playthings eat

the shouting children. No, and the glass white
televised cathedral?—that
was a sight seen for the sin-
gle flashed moment, and gone.

I saw the tar-pits at La Brea,
where a dark endowed museum squats, and where
the thick blots of lake are watched,
and the haired replicas stroked and touched

by kiddies. There's a tour:
the intelligible stone, the Short-Faced Bear,
the Dire Wolf, American Lion and Mastodon,
and Man with not much brain.

Well they did all make a dumb
choice that day! But my day was warm
and fascinating. Try to see these
tar-pits, in La Brea, in Los Angeles.

Gary Margolis

The Human Cannon Ball climbs down into
　　the barrel of the cannon, safe in the tube's
darkness, waiting, like me, for the film to punch
　　him up the metal shaft and into the canvas

air, down-tent, to the inflated landing bag.
　　I'm holding my breath because a pair
of purple finches have nested in the exploding
　　fuschia next to the door and are gun-shy

when anyone comes or goes, so their young
　　are fed more on my family's comings and
goings than their own hunger. Mother
　　flits from the willow to the box elder,

waiting for evening, for a lull long enough
　　to poke a seed into a new throat. So I
ask everyone to use the back door which is
　　easy to forget to do and not to scent the nest

with our kind, out of curiosity or the wish
　　to kiss a berry into one of the four blind
gaping mouths. Father, rosy and raspberry,
　　not purple, stays on a near branch, as if

• • •

standing on a spring, waiting to see if I will
　　have the courage to breathe, when the Human
Cannon Ball is launched into the air
　　and turns himself like a maple leaf, a snow

goose feathering into a corn field, toward
　　the arms of the audience, which can never
take the place of the pink blown-up plastic
　　bag that will save him a few frames and words

from now—if I can stand here, still as a shadow
　　of a nest, breathing like the wind that flies
through the weedy branches of the box elder,
　　here, empty as the air that needs to take him up.

Robert Shaw

Thinking about them as you saw them last,
you see them standing there behind your back,
leaning out into the road to wave goodbye,
lingering even as growing speed and distance
diminish them until they neatly fit
head to foot in the mirror-strip you glance at.
Tiny in your lengthening wake, still waving,
they could be nameless people on a postcard,
too far away for you to make out faces.
Then, at the first turn, they're lost completely,
places taken by someone's windbreak pines,
a split-rail fence, and then, as the wheel straightens,
nothing but empty road. Ahead of you
are towns where you will never know a soul,
exits following exits you will pass
and never take, amassing a stiff toll
finally to make good on. Fortunately
you carry along with you that higher-powered
reflective instrument that you can use
no matter how far down the road you've gone
to bring them back in view as large as life,
putting yourself in the picture, too, which makes
thinking about them as you saw them lasting.

Yehuda Amichai

Two disappeared into a house.
The marble of the stairs comforts the feet of those who ascend
as it comforts the feet of those who descend,
like the marble that comforts the dead in their graves.
And the higher the stairs, the less worn they are,
the highest are like new
for the souls that leave no footprints.
Like people who live in the high country:
when they speak, their voices grow more songful
up to the singing of the heavenly angels.

Two disappeared into a house
turn on a light. Then turn it off.
The stairs go out from the roof into
the space of night
as in a building that was never finished.

Translated by Chana Bloch and Stephen Mitchell

Virginia Hamilton Adair

Stunted bush
beside the unpaved road
the shepherd often passes here
with his hundred sheep
their hooves churning the soft sand
the lambs bouncing as they follow along.

We walked under the palms
to see the shepherd lead
his traveling company
but they had gone by earlier
the dust had settled.

Under the stunted bush
a cool hollow in the sand
in it a lamb too lame to follow
a lamb with its feet wired together
lifted its little face.

Mark Halliday

The young guy at the register in FoodTek
scratches under his Runnin' Rebels hat
while talking on the phone while selling pastries.
It is all casual and okay. I might purchase
an almond crescent. I might not.
Commerce thrives. Eleven p.m. commerce
thrives on South Street all casual it's culture
in motion. Which hats, which teeshirts,
which band upstairs at Bad Rooster,
which Turf Tuff Sting Pipe Steak Blacking motorcycles,
which thin quick girl-woman with violet hair
who makes me old-sad with my coffee.
With my late hazelnut coffee in FoodTek.
Everything all okay and casual and the guy
selling pastries while talking on the phone
scratches under his Runnin' Rebels hat
all just a typical night of commerce
night of culture just typically thriving.
I sit here I sit here I sit here it's one of those
here I sit situations, no violet girl at this table
here and when another man writes this kind of poem
I think it's pathetic. When any other man writes this
here-I-sit stuff I promptly want to be fast-casual
or violet-strange. But it's me
here. Might ask for an almond crescent, might not,

. . .

and the guy with the Runnin' Rebels hat
would be hypersensitized if he noticed
while selling and talking that I (here sit I) here
with my helpless late refusal-of-sleep hazelnut coffee
have floated past midpoint, even far past midpoint
down the damply central river of me
sitting with my metaphor and hazelnut coffee late

and the current all casual
accelerating so softly
as I let it happen
in FoodTek on a winter night in '94
and him still on the phone about somebody's overdue rent.

Dean Young

People are compelled to be together good and bad.
You've agreed to shrimp with the geology couple.
If you like one 85% and the other 35%
that's not so bad.
You need to like one at least 70%
and like the other not less than 25%
otherwise it's agonizing and pointless
like being crucified without religious significance.
Averages are misleading:
I like that couple 110% could mean
each is appreciated 55% which will not kill you
but neither will sleeping in your own urine.
One should like oneself between 60 and 80%.
Under 45%, one becomes an undertaking,
prone to eating disorders, public weeping,
useless for gift wrapping and relay races.
Over 85% means you are a self-involved bore,
I don't care about your Nobel Prize in positrons
or your dog sled victories.
Of course there is great variance throughout the day.
You may feel 0% upon first waking
but that is because you don't yet know you exist
which is why baby-studies have been a bust.
Then as you venture forth to boil water,
you may feel a sudden surge to 90%,

Hey, I'm GOOD at boiling water!
which can be promptly counteracted by turning on your e-mail.
It is important not to let variance become too extreme,
a range of 40% is allowable,
beyond that it is as great storms upon drought-stricken land.
I.e. mudslides.
Sugar, retirement plans, impending jail time
all are influential factors.
Generally, most data has been gathered
regarding raising percentages,
the modern world it is argued is plentiful
with opportunities of negative effect.
The tanker splits and the shore birds turn black and lose their
    ability to float.
Sometimes a good scrub is all that's needed.
A fresh shirt.
Shock therapy has never been fully discounted
and people have felt significant surges
from backpacking into remote and elevated areas,
a call home.
Yet the very same may backfire.
Thwamp, thwamp, the helicopter lowers the rescue crew,
the phone slammed down.
Each case is profoundly nuanced.
like the lock systems of Holland.

Some, frankly, are beyond help,
but if you are a tall woman, wear shoes to make you taller!
Candy corn, what kind of person doesn't like candy corn?
Tell that 70 / 35% rock couple you can not come,
you forgot your fencing lesson,
your cat just had a puppy,
your tongue is green,
you are in fact dying.

Tom Clark

Little Prince basks serene
As an Egyptian god on his barge
On the green cushion, gently breathing

While in his sleep mouselike plays the mind
With its empty toys less real
Than the large drops of rain the nightwind tosses

The night, dark as the flooding of the Nile
The brain, that clouded crystal ball
Blurry with drowned thoughts—

A waterlogged squirrel that gathers
Its nuts to float this dream of words sub noctis
From *magic* to *error*, from *aether* to *terra*

On the upriver stream toward morning

Adam Zagajewski

IRON TRAIN | 137

The train stopped at a little station
and for a moment stood absolutely still.
The doors slammed, gravel crunched underfoot,
someone said goodbye forever,

a glove dropped, the sun dimmed,
the doors slammed again, even louder,
and the iron train set off slowly
and vanished in the fog like the nineteenth century.

Translated by Clare Cavanagh

Timothy Steele

We'd not have guessed that we'd be heartened so
To see this snowshoe rabbit, months from snow,

Come from the woods with that shy tread of his,
Drawn by our bushy rows of lettuces,

His summer coat all rich soft grays and browns,
His feet as overstated as a clown's.

How delicate he is: he holds no brief
For this or that variety of leaf,

But tries each, crouching as a cat will do
Before a dinner bowl and, when he's through,

Slips back across the grasses gingerly
(Binoculars enable us to see

The crickets that his cautious lopings flush)
And vanishes into the underbrush.

Robert Morgan

Remembering the descriptions by Wilson
and Bartram, and Audubon and other
early travelers to the interior, of the sky
clouded with the movements of winged pilgrims
wide as the Mississippi, wide as the Gulf
Stream, hundred-mile epics of equidistant wings
horizon to horizon, how their droppings
splashed the lakes and rivers, how
where they roosted whole forests broke down
worse than from ice storms, and the woods floor
was paved with their lime, how the settlers
got them with ax and gun and broom
for hogs, how when a hawk attacked
the endless stream bulged away
and kept the shift long after
the raptor was gone, and having read how
the skies of America became silent, the fletched
oceans forgotten, how can I replace
the hosts of the sky, the warm-blooded jetstreams?
To echo the birdstorms of those early
sunsets, what high river of electron, cell and star?

Don McKay

Here's to your good looks and the neat way you shit
with a brisk bob like a curtsey, easy as song.
Here's to your song, which,
though "neither rhythmical nor musical" (*The Birds of Canada*),
relieves me of all speech and never deals with what is past,
or passing, or to come.
And, as a monument to the sturdy fragile woven
scrotum of your nest,
I hereby dedicate baseball.

Eamon Grennan

The dead bee lies on the window ledge, a relic,
its amber-yellow body barred in black and its head

tucked in, dust gathering on every follicle
and on the geodesic dome of the head—all tucked in

and tucked away, so neat is death. And the many
flies too, all sizes, lying on their sides as if

asleep, just a quick nap and they'll be up and off
about their business. Souls, we used to say:

bees, butterflies, moths, wasps, all sorts of flies,
the air crowded and loud with leftover angels—

but not the spider in its complex web, fallen
from grace but walking on air, vigilant in ways

that harden the heart, getting its appetite back.

Philip Memmer

for Franz-Peter Griesmaier

My philosopher friend is explaining again
that the bottle of well-chilled beer in my hand

might not be a bottle of beer,
that the trickle of bottle-sweat cooling my palm

might not be wet, might not be cool,
that in fact it's impossible ever to know

if I'm holding a bottle at all.
I try to follow his logic, flipping the steaks

that are almost certainly hissing
over the bed of coals—coals I'd swear

were black at first, then gray, then red—
coals we could spread out and walk on

and why not, I ask, since we'll never be sure
if our feet burn, if our soles

blister and peel, if our faithlessness
is any better or worse a tool

than the firewalker's can-do extreme.
Exactly, he smiles. Behind the fence

the moon rises, or seems to.
Have another. Whatever else is true,

the coals feel hotter than ever
as the darkness begins to do

what darkness does. *Another what?* I ask.

Ron Padgett

Now honorable leg broken.
The fog drifts over the docks.
It is a terrible movie
I can't watch, but I do.
Charlie goes into the next room
and removes his hat: ladies.
They fuss and fret, but Charlie
shows them his broken leg
and receives honorable sympathy.
His son dashes in: Dad,
come quick! Charlie tells ladies:
Do not leave room please.
Their fluttering flustered looks
bounce off the walls, which
change from medium gray
to pulsating red. Charlie peeps
in door, says, Red good luck.

Catherine Doty

Every day, our mother says,
kids die on those goddamned things,
and she nods at the lone yellow horse
with the red vinyl bridle
and four black, shining hooves
like police hat brims.
Not only do we stop our five-part
begging, we walk wide around the beast,
though Mary brushes the coin box
with her sleeve.

Rigid in flight, the great horse's legs
flange out toward us. Not one of us argues.
We hold onto our mother's coat, cross
several streets, touch the dog we always touch
when we walk home, fingering
his freckled snout. Then we scream
and run in the yard while supper cooks,
and the sky shudders pale for some seconds
before it darkens, as if in that lavender moment,
three blocks away, a child drops
the reins and gasps as his shoes fly off,
and plumes of smoke rise
from the crown of his hand-knit hat.

Ben Howard

What better place to set down furtive thoughts
than here at the Imperial Hotel
on Denny Street at seven in the morning?
Not so much imperial as mellow
and darkened by Victorian décor,
this dining room is vacant but for us,
that harried-looking waiter and the one
he waits on, namely me. As for the notes
I'm writing over tea too hot to swallow
and toast that leaves its relics on my palate,
I see them as a sieve, through which the faint
odor of last night's fish, the kitchen clatter,
the muted talk of patrons in the lobby,
and all the sights I have or haven't noted
are passing to their final destination.
But even as I mutter my lament
for all things left unrecognized, unnoticed,
I'm thinking of the Sunday afternoon
I pulled a yellowed journal from the shelf
and found in it the features of a dream
of which I had no other recollection,
no tension in the limbs or in the heart.
If it survives, that story of a ride
through empty streets in someone else's car,
it's in those sentences, themselves imperiled.

Lift up your voices, cries the aging hymn.
Lift up your cameras, your pens and notebooks,
lest the images that flash and fade—
that taut inflection in a fleeting voice—
be no more lasting than a passing thought
and no less formless than a jotted dream.

Michael Donaghy

LOCAL 32B | 146

(US National Union of Building Service Workers)

The rich are different. Where we have doorknobs,
they have doormen—like me, a cigar store Indian
on the Upper East Side, in polyester, in August.
As the tenants tanned in Tenerife and Monaco
I stood guard beneath Manhattan's leaden light
watching poodle turds bake grey in half an hour.
Another hot one, Mr Rockefeller!
An Irish doorman foresees his death,
waves, and runs to help it with its packages.
Once I got a cab for Pavarotti. No kidding.
No tip either. I stared after him down Fifth
and caught him looking after me, then through me,
like Samson, eyeless, at the Philistine chorus—
Yessir, I put the tenor in the vehicle.
And a mighty tight squeeze it was.

Kim Addonizio

CHICKEN | 147

Why did she cross the road?
She should have stayed in her little cage,
shat upon by her sisters above her,
shitting on her sisters below her.

God knows how she got out.
God sees everything. God has his eye
on the chicken, making her break
like the convict headed for the river,

sloshing his way through the water
to throw off the dogs, raising
his arms to starlight to praise
whatever isn't locked in a cell.

He'll make it to a farmhouse
where kind people will feed him.
They'll bring green beans and bread,
home-brewed hops. They'll bring

the chicken the farmer found
by the side of the road, dazed
from being clipped by a pickup,
whose delicate brain stem

. . .

he snapped with a twist,
whose asshole his wife stuffed
with rosemary and a lemon wedge.
Everything has its fate,

but only God knows what that is.
The spirit of the chicken will enter the convict.
Sometimes, in his boxy apartment,
listening to his neighbors above him,

annoying his neighbors below him,
he'll feel a terrible hunger
and an overwhehning urge
to jab his head at the television over and over.

Kerry Hardie

It was January,
I'd hardly seen anyone for days, you understand.
The sheep were all sitting separate and silent,
a hard wind was coming in over the hill,
a white moon floated.

I'd bought the pumpkin for soup.
My arms had dropped with the weight of it,
dropped and come back, like the bounce back up into air
after the deep of the river.
I'd hefted it in from the car,
set it down on the table.
It was smaller and fiercer and redder than I'd expected.

I was out on the hill for the sake of the moon
and the ash trees, raking the way with shadow.
Where the road ran high the fields slid into the valley.
Cloud covered the slopes of the mountains,
laying down snow.
I carried the color, red fire on the dark of the table,
the color would bear me through till his return.

• • •

When I got home the phone was ringing,
I had the key in the door but it wouldn't turn.
I heard the phone cease in the empty house.
And the dogs milled about.
And the pumpkin stared out at the moon.

Bob Hicok

TO ROANOKE WITH
JOHNNY CASH | 149

Mist became rain became fog was mist
reborn every few miles on a road
made of s and z, of switchback

and falling into mountains of night
would have been easy and who
would have known until flames

and nobody, even then. I played his life
over and over, not so much song
as moan of a needle and the bite,

the hole it eats through the arm
and drove faster to the murmur
of this dead and crow-dressed man,

voice of prison and heroin and the bible
as turned by murdering hands.
And the road was the color of him

• • •

and the night was blind but the mist
turned blaze in headlights as I haunted
myself with one of the last songs

he sang, about what else, about pain
and death and regret and the fall
that was the soul of the man.

Joseph Harrison

AIR LARRY | 150

*(Larry Walters flew a lawn chair attached to helium
balloons to a height of 16,000 feet, into the jet lanes above
Los Angeles; he named his craft "Inspiration I.")*

When the idea came
It seemed, at best, a dicey thing to do:
You rig your vehicle, give it a name,
Straighten a line or two,

Then, confident you've given it your best
If not that it will carry you aloft,
You put it to the test
And it just takes off,

Lifting you over the trees
And up the sky
Easy as you please,
Till soon you are really high,

Your neighborhood, turned miniature, is gone,
And you wonder how,
Up here all alone,
To get the hell down, now

That the transcendental imagination
Has proven it can indeed

Surpass your wildest expectation
And raise you higher than you need

Or want to go,
For now that you are "there"
All you know is how little you know,
And that here in the upper air

It is very cold,
A disenabling extremity
Your clumsy calculations should have foretold,
And, triggering all your anxiety,

You hear, then see, roaring across the sky
As dots in the distance streak into form,
The gargantuan craft come cruising by,
Perfectly uniform,

Built for speed and altitude,
So effortless in shattering sound itself
That next to them your vehicle looks crude
And fatally flawed, just like yourself,

Painfully ill-equipped to play the hero,
And actually beginning to freeze to death

At a temperature far below zero
Where the thin air burns each breath,

And you realize you must, not a moment too soon,
Jettison all original intent
And pop your own balloon
To undertake the perilous descent.

Philip Dacey

THOMAS EAKINS:
A DREAM OF POWERS | 151

As to Eakins painting nude young males, he no doubt would have painted a female "Swimming Hole" if he could have.

—Gordon Hendricks, *The Life and Work of Thomas Eakins*

I'm both painting "The Swimming Hole" and in it, too,
except the sex is all wrong. Five of the Academy's
female students are having a bathing party,

their many-layered clothes piled on the green
triangle of grass in the lower, lefthand corner.
A picnic basket sits on the stone jetty.

And now I'm painting in—because it's there
by the basket—a bottle of wine, half-filled,
a sunshot deep red, central brilliance. But where

are the glasses? Pursed lips draw from the bottle.
I tell my models to stop moving about so much
and assume the same poses as their male

counterparts, but they just laugh off such
heresy, plant fists on hips and, grinning, hiss.
Unlike the men, all separate, the women touch

• • •

each other: one who's taken the dripping tresses
of another in her hands supports with her back
a third leaning against her to practice

ballet steps. There's a diver here, too, but—look!—
she's doing a backflip. How'd such muscular legs
develop in Philadelphia? No doubt the work

of wearing all those clothes, their heft and drag.
I think of escaped genies relishing their freedom—
Harry barks at the airborne body as his dog-

paddle turns thrash—and wonder what's to become
of my pyramidal design. These powers mad
for the future surely won't go back where they came from,

into tight spaces of any sort, but rather mean to add
curve upon curve, conceiving circles that open
wide like arms to embrace the surrounding woods.

Only one bather has remained still. It's Susan!
Hands under her head, eyes closed, she rests
on her back, and I love her for the first time again,

• • •

pierced by the way her ankles coolly cross.
That's me in the blond wig, the uninvited guest,
up to my neck, hiding my lack of breasts.

Bill Knott

Fingerprints look like ripples
because time keeps dropping
another stone into our palm.

Ron Padgett

Nothing in that drawer.
Nothing in that drawer.
Nothing in that drawer.
Nothing in that drawer.
Nothing in that drawer.
Nothing in that drawer.
Nothing in that drawer.
Nothing in that drawer.
Nothing in that drawer.
Nothing in that drawer.
Nothing in that drawer.
Nothing in that drawer.
Nothing in that drawer.
Nothing in that drawer.

Linda Pastan

We roll up rugs and strip the beds by rote,
summer expires as it has done before.
The ferry is no simple pleasure boat

nor are we simply cargo, though we'll float
alongside heavy trucks—their stink and roar.
We roll up rugs and strip the beds by rote.

This bit of land whose lines the glaciers wrote
becomes the muse of memory once more;
the ferry is no simple pleasure boat.

I'll trade my swimsuit for a woolen coat;
the torch of autumn has but small allure.
We roll up rugs and strip the beds by rote.

The absences these empty shells denote
suggest the losses winter has in store.
The ferry is no simple pleasure boat.

The songs of summer dwindle to one note:
the fog horn's blast (which drowns this closing door).
We rolled up rugs and stripped the beds by rote.
The ferry is no simple pleasure boat.

Timothy Steele

Our jet storms down the runway, tilts up, lifts:
We're airborne, and each second we see more—
Outlying hangars, wetlands with a pond
That flashes like sheened silver and, beyond,
An estuary and the frozen drifts
Of breakers wide and white along a shore.

One watches, cheek in palm. How little weight
The world has as it swiftly drops away!
How quietly the mind climbs to this height
As now, the seat-belt sign turned off, a flight
Attendant rises to negotiate
The steep aisle to a curtained service bay.

James Tate

I was evidently just staring into space.
I had gone downtown for something and couldn't
remember what it was. I know it had seemed
important at the time. A man I knew slightly,
but whose name escaped me, if I ever knew it at
all, said to me, "Hey, Luther, what have you
been up to lately?" I was startled but tried
not to show it. "Oh, busy as usual. Too much
work, not enough time. How about yourself?" I
said. "Oh, Crystal and I did manage to go camp-
ing for a week recently. It rained most of the
time, but still we had a great time. Crystal
always asks about you," he said. "She does?"
I said. "Sure. She thinks you're a great guy.
You should come over for dinner some time. She'll
cook you a great meal. Take care, pal, I gotta
run," he said. "Yeah, take care, good to see
you," I said. I watched him disappear down the
street. Quite a stride, definitely a man on a
mission. I like that, well, sort of. Brad and
Crystal Austin—I met them at Renata's party

several years ago. They talked about their sublime villa in Tuscany all night until I was nearly comatose. Flashlight batteries and toothpaste, these were all I needed for the good life.

William Stafford

AT THE UN-NATIONAL MONUMENT
ALONG THE CANADIAN BORDER | 157

This is the field where the battle did not happen,
where the unknown soldier did not die.
This is the field where grass joined hands,
where no monument stands,
and the only heroic thing is the sky.

Birds fly here without any sound,
unfolding their wings across the open.
No people killed—or were killed—on this ground
hallowed by neglect and an air so tame
that people celebrate it by forgetting its name.

Stuart Dybek

The third rail
and the electric chair

are charged with the current
that glows tonight

in the bedside lamp
illuminating your body.

Ron Koertge

OFF-TRACK BETTING | 159

I always shave and shine my shoes. I'm young
enough to read the *Racing Form* with drug
store cheaters, not like Immense Jerome
across the way who squints and feels the print

like it was Braille. And cashes, anyway.
Nobody beats the races. Its mysteries
are too demure. Still, it's fun to lure
some friends from chilly Aqueduct

to Tampa Bay and swear in Spanish for
a change. It's fun to eye the random
girl in faded, low-slung jeans by Jeopardy
yet be enamored by this bulky maiden

field from Finger Lakes. The favorite
looks badly frayed. Dear God, is this the day
that off-the-shoulder gown of Chance
falls to the bedroom floor at last?

"One minute to the post!" I bet the farm.
My blood accelerates. I light the single
cigarette that I'm allowed. The crowd
opens its beery mouth and roars as some

• • •

old gelding remembers how it's done.
The board lights up at nine-to-one. I go
to take a leak. It hurts to pee sometimes.
My heart feels weird. Ah, screw it. I'm on

their money. The light looks like melted cheese,
which I still want. I'll buy a round instead.
I'll tell a joke. Upstairs, there's nine to go,
the last a mortal lock from Pimlico.

Donald Justice

UNFLUSHED URINALS | 160

lines written in the Omaha bus station

Seeing them, I recognize the contempt
Some men have for themselves.

This man, for instance, zipping quickly up, head turned,
Like a bystander innocent of his own piss.

And here comes one to repair himself at the mirror,
Patting down damp, sparse hairs, suspiciously still black,
Poor bantam cock of a man, jaunty at one a.m., perfumed,
    undiscourageable . . .

O the saintly forbearance of these mirrors!
The acceptingness of the washbowls, in which we absolve
    ourselves!

birthdays you bend and blow
out a candle in a skull

it's always just one candle
but each year one more

skull is added to the table
which by now is plus full

and that makes this ritual
more impossible each year

each year as you approach
that crowd of past selves

somewhere down there
in all those bone sockets

the annual candle waiting
glares and dares you to find it

Diane Thiel

After a line from a Russian song

If you don't have a dog
your neighbor will not poison it

and if you don't have a home
you will not have to run from it

when your father's anger shakes the walls
that don't exist because you don't have a home

to grow up in—nowhere to learn
that the husband you won't have

won't leave you for another woman
won't walk out your door one morning—

because you won't have a door
for anyone to leave or enter through

and you won't have a window
for anyone to see you

. . .

and if you don't make plans
they will not need to be changed

like the diapers you won't change
since you won't have a child

who will never change your life
whose tiny fingers you will never hold

because of how hard you never wished
and planned her away so many times

and she won't grow up to hate you
for everything you never did

as if you didn't have a child—and she won't learn
that if you don't have a memory

the past cannot devour you
when you stop moving for a brief

moment. Long enough to let the sorrow
catch the joy you never feel because you

• • •

don't want to feel the sorrow
its companion. And if you don't feel—

there will be nothing left to heal.

Thomas Lux

which he must
cross, by swimming, for fruit and nuts,
to help him
I sit, with my rifle, on a platform
high in a tree, same side of the river
as the hungry monkey. How does this assist
him? When he swims for it
I look first up river: predators move faster with
the current than against it.
If a crocodile is aimed from up river to eat the monkey
and an anaconda from down river burns
with the same ambition, I do
the math, algebra, angles, rate-of-monkey
croc and snake-speed, and if, *if*
it looks like the anaconda or the croc
will reach the monkey
before he attains the river's far bank,
I raise my rifle and fire
one, two, three, even four times, into the river
just behind the monkey
to hurry him up a little.

Shoot the snake, the crocodile?
They're just doing their jobs,
but the monkey, the monkey
has little hands, like a child's
and the smart ones, in a cage, can be taught to smile.

Virginia Hamilton Adair

Where did I leave off yesterday?
I stood at midnight with the mouse
caught in a cornflake box and rustling slightly.
What to do next? I stepped outside
into the backdoor tangle of thorns and roses.
I did not know my neighbors.
They'd be puzzled to see a cereal box
in their backyard. Good luck,
little mouse, I said, as the box sailed
over the high fence.

Our next mouse crept
into an empty cider jug for the sweet dreg.
I stood the bottle up, a sad, sweet jail.
Almost at once she gave birth to a litter of six.
I carried the bottle of mice to Lincoln Park
and left the jug on its side, for easy exit,
under a sheltering bush. They were all
Beatrix Potter mice, dainty and lovable;
not the gross travesties of Disney.

         I was lonely
with my husband away all day at work.
But after a wild party Kentucky Derby Day,
we too began to breed in Rapley Caves, under our thicket of
  pipes

but not in a cereal box or cider bottle.
In the first cyclone to hit the eastern mid-Atlantic coast,
we moved to New Haven in such a deluge
that canoes passed us on the Boston Post Road,
and driving into New Haven,
all the elms blew down behind us.
I survived a surfeit of tainted oysters
and gave birth to our first child.
He will be 55 next week.

Why am I telling you all this?

Jane Kenyon

There's just no accounting for happiness,
or the way it turns up like a prodigal
who comes back to the dust at your feet
having squandered a fortune far away.

And how can you not forgive?
You make a feast in honor of what
was lost, and take from its place the finest
garment, which you saved for an occasion
you could not imagine, and you weep night and day
to know that you were not abandoned,
that happiness saved its most extreme form
for you alone.

No, happiness is the uncle you never
knew about, who flies a single-engine plane
onto the grassy landing strip, hitchhikes
into town, and inquires at every door
until he finds you asleep midafternoon
as you so often are during the unmerciful
hours of your despair.

It comes to the monk in his cell.
It comes to the woman sweeping the street
with a birch broom, to the child

whose mother has passed out from drink.
It comes to the lover, to the dog chewing
a sock, to the pusher, to the basket maker,
and to the clerk stacking cans of carrots
in the night.
      It even comes to the boulder
in the perpetual shade of pine barrens,
to rain falling on the open sea,
to the wineglass, weary of holding wine.

Charles Simic

You must come to them sideways
In rooms webbed in shadow,
Sneak a view of their emptiness
Without them catching
A glimpse of you in return.

The secret is,
Even the empty bed is a burden to them,
A pretense.
They are more themselves keeping
The company of a blank wall,
The company of time and eternity

Which, begging your pardon,
Cast no image
As they admire themselves in the mirror,
While you stand to the side
Pulling a hanky out
To wipe your brow surreptitiously.

Tony Towle

the Mona Lisa, in the Village
at Bleecker and Seventh, a blip
from the middle ages
on the radar screen
of that young woman over there,
while she thinks of someone else.

I should have brought
something to read
because I have nothing to do now but write,
the way I used to
forty years ago, in the Figaro,
in the Village
at MacDougal and Bleecker, exhilarated
by loneliness, poverty, and paralyzing
indecision, and resolutely ignoring the fact
that everyone cool in there
could tell that I wasn't—
lost to what was *happening*
behind the overpriced coffee, 35 cents
for the fuel
to infiltrate oblivion;

and I waited for a girlfriend
and composed jejune little ironies

that I hoped would pass for poems,
and I had all the time in the world.

I could see the San Remo bar across the street
where I learned years later
real New York poets went
and drank real drinks;
but the San Remo has since disappeared
with everything else from 1960—
discarded, lost, or broken, or certainly
wouldn't fit me anymore,
except the sound advice
still gathering dust:

Think before you speak.
(Yes, I probably should have done that.)
A penny saved is a penny earned.
(That could have been made a bit clearer, perhaps.)
Don't be a complete idiot.
(Hey, I gave it a shot.)
You really should think about a career.
I'm thinking about it now
and there it is: involuntary barbs,
unasked-for opinions

and missed opportunities strewn
and rusting about the incorporeal field.

I told Diane I'd be here 'til six. Waiting
for a girlfriend *literally* is a great improvement
over afternoons at the Figaro;
and in fact it's cool to *have* a girlfriend at my age
I think amusedly to myself
behind the overpriced coffee,
2.95 to contemplate the traffic
fleeing down Seventh and into the past,
which brings me up to the present,
where I put down my pen, figuratively.

Dan Gerber

It occurs to you that everything has gone awry.
It all should have turned out differently.
Everyone has chosen the wrong mate. Everything
that should have been spoken has been restrained.
It's not the world but the residue of what the
world intended. It all makes sense to you, now
that your mistresses have gotten married. Eternity.
We are living in eternity.

The clouds break open, the sun about to set.
Nothing you can do about it. You walk from your
hotel, down rain-washed streets, glistening in places.
The cafés are closed, or you feel they should
be closed. The life in them doesn't concern you.
Exhausted by certainty, nothing concerns you
but the pull of the river, the dark
brown current swirling in eddies, drawn too
powerfully to what it doesn't know, not to turn
back on itself. You watch a glassy ring, watch it
ripple then curl, till it's lost in the stream.
And you notice the pavement under your feet, the
hardness of it, and of the iron rail under your arms.

Pattiann Rogers

The easy parting of oaks and hickories,
bays of willows, borders of pine and screens
of bamboo down to the crux, grasses, bulrushes
and reeds parting down to their fundamental
cores, the yielding of murky pond waters,
layer upon layer giving way to the touch

of the right touch, the glassy, clear
spring waters, bone and gristle alike
opening as if opening were ultimate fact,
the parting of reflection allowing passage,
and the cold, amenable skeleton of echo,
the unlatching of *marsh* becoming as easily

accessible as the unlocking of *mercy*,
as the revelation of stone splitting
perfectly with the sound of the right
sound, everything, a nubbin of corn,
a particle of power, the epiphany of the sky
relenting, and the sea swinging open

• • •

like doors of a theater giving entrance
to everyone, no fences, no barriers, no blinds
to the parting of the abyss, not bolted,
not barred from the utmost offering
of the dusk, enigma itself falling away
until all may enter all and pass among them.

Abigail Gramig

Today
is the
perfect day

The sky
just so
clouds moving
fast

Drops of water
on leaves
of Russian sage

Dog sitting
her chin
on crossed paws

Light streams
through branches
of locust tree

I sit
just so
at the
small table

. . .

Everything is
perfect
just like this
you would have said

Philip Nikolayev

The cold March afternoon waxed languid
with its late hours. The cinders sang
their lowpitched ancient fireplace ditty
with an insufferable hang.

I wasn't sleepy. On the table
there sat potato chips galore
with Morellino de Scansano,
vintage of 1994.

Fingers of shadow played obscurely
behind the weakened flames. Blasé,
the Christmas cactus nodded mildly
like an art dealer from LA.

And I, with no premeditation,
returned the Shelley to the shelf,
unwound sublimely on the sofa,
lit up a cig and shot myself.

Aidan Rooney-Céspedes

Bungalows, God said, Day 1, and up they sprang like
    buttercups:
with lawns and railings, gate; three bedrooms off a hall; a
    phone that squats
on the hall-stand; back door, scullery, red formica
    countertops.

Day 2, God dollied in the stove, and rigged the central heating.
The oil-man came and fired her up; but God saw that a cold
    feeling
lingered, and called for back-boilers, slack, aeroboard on the
    ceiling.

Volkswagens, He said, Day 3, to get people out to do a run,
round the relatives, Armagh for butter, daytrips to Bundoran,
and once a year, two weeks down south, Courtown, Lahinch,
    Ballybunion

where He made, Day 4, Strand Hotels, sandy beaches, buckets
    'n' spades,
souvenir rock to strengthen teeth, a cliff walk, a straw hat,
    promenades,
donkey rides, pitch 'n' putt, a machine to roll pennies in
    arcades.

• • •

And God saw that all this was good, if thirsty, work; so God
    made fondness
Day 5, and put a few pubs in every street. Next He made
    Guinness,
whiskey, gin, vodka, minerals. Then, nite-clubs to extend
    business

till all hours of Day 6: takeaways, coffee-shops, supermarkets,
99s, crispy pancakes, Tayto, Co-Op milk and custard yogurts,
squirty tomatoes, organic courgettes, kiwis, kitchen gadgets.

Day 7: Mass; said by Himself, and after that, *The Sunday Tribune,*
again, mostly about Himself, His enterprise—the good wine all
    gone,
His mangled talents rusting by slow rivers, His manna eaten,

and all His marvels dead, His oceans rising, hell-bent to
    Heaven.

Bill Knott

THE FATE | 173

for Anne-Marie Stretter

Standing on the youthhold I saw a shooting star
And knew it predestined encounter with the sole love
But that comet crashed into the earth so hard
Tilted its axis a little bit not much just enough
To make me miss meeting her by one or two yards.

Linda Pastan

In starched dresses
with ribbons
in miniature jackets
and tiny ties
we would circle
the chairs
at birthday parties and
when the music
stopped, lunge
to be seated. One
by one we were welcomed
to hard ground
and empty air.

Robin Robertson

I am used to the smell by now,
the stillness, these shifts
in waist measurement,
the bad skin. But my hair
is lustrous, the cheekbones
well-defined, and my nails,
it seems, still growing.

Wisława Szymborska

THE FIRST PHOTOGRAPH
OF HITLER | 176

And who is this baby in a robe?
Why, it's little Dolphie, the son of Mr. and Mrs. Hitler!
Perhaps he'll grow up to be a doctor of law?
Or he'll be a tenor in the Vienna Opera?
Whose tiny hand is it, whose tiny ear, eye, nose?
Whose little belly full of milk, we don't know yet:
A printer, councillor, merchant, priest?
Where will these funny legs take him, where to?
To a garden, a school, the office, a wedding,
perhaps with the mayor's daughter?

Sweet tot, little angel, crumb, tiny ray of light,
when he was coming into this world a year ago,
there was no lack of signs in heaven and earth:
Spring sun, geraniums in windows,
music of organ-grinders in the courtyard,
auspicious omen in pink tissue paper,
prophetic dream of the mother just before the delivery:
To see a dove in a dream—good news,
to catch this dove—a long-awaited guest will arrive.
Knock, knock, who's there? So beats Dolphie's tiny heart.

Pacifier, diapers, bib, rattle,
the boy, thank God!, knock on wood, is healthy,

looks like his parents, like a pussycat in a basket
like children from all other family albums.

Well, we probably won't cry now,
Mister Photographer will go click under his black hood.
Studio Klinger, Grabenstrasse Braumen,
and Braumen is a small but dignified town,
solid firms, decent neighbors,
smell of dough rising, and grey soap.
One hears neither the howling of dogs nor the steps of
       destiny.

The history teacher loosens his collar
and yawns over the students' notebooks.

Translated by Stanislaw Baranczak and Clare Cavanagh

Gregory Djanikian

THE SOLDIERS | 177

Their cruelty toward the victims grew greater as their physical sufferings grew more intense.

—*Arnold Toynbee*

They took him out to the pasture
and shot him, a bullet
to the back of the head,

and the death was instant
but it wasn't enough,
they weren't satisfied,

so they cut off his hands
for safekeeping,
they ripped out his beard

and threw it to the wind
like shed fur from an animal,
and they said they felt better now,

too bad they hadn't done it
sooner, when it counted,
though something else

• • •

was making them irritable,
his looking through them maybe
with the densest eyes,

so they took the eyes,
and then the ears too
as if he could hear their laughter,

and then they decided
why not take the face,
the whole of it,

and they did, in one piece,
and left him open
and tipped to the sky

so that his daughters,
finding him like that,
faceless, barely himself,

were almost unable
to weep or anoint with oil
or to say this is ours

. . .

until they had turned him over,
put him face down, the blood
draining into the dirt,

and the body, as if asleep
and unremarkable, looking
like all the others now.

Oliver Rice

TIMELY ENUMERATIONS
CONCERNING SRI LANKA | 178

Those are the central mountains,
the surrounding plains,
the coasts of mangrove, lagoon, river delta.

This is the temple compound
where the rite will begin this morning
exactly at the hour of Buddha's enlightenment.

A muttering rises from the roadway
where already, the curfew lifted,
the prawn sellers are out.

That is a tea estate,
a rubber,
a coconut,
where coolies live and die.
There is a graphite mine
where they dig on their knees.

This is the assistant in the ceremony arriving,
who otherwise drives a three wheel taxi,
and these are the brushes, the paints,
the ritual mirror he bears.

• • •

The koha birds begin their proclamations
to the boutiques in the new town,
the tenements in the old town,
to the enclaves of the Tamil Hindu minority,
the Sinhalese Buddhist majority.

Those are the relics of the Portuguese occupation,
the Dutch,
the British,
of the struggle for independence.

Here is the ladder propped before the sculpture,
and this is the artist, regally attired,
climbing meticulously, rung by rung,
his back to the carving,
who otherwise keeps records for the tax collector.

The sun rises again on the headlines,
the beggars at the railroad station,
the fish drying on the beach.

Those are the sites of bloodshed
between the government and the insurgents,
villages where massacres have occurred,

rooms where captives were tortured,
grounds where they were surreptitiously buried.

This is the assistant holding the mirror
for the artist to view the stone face,
and here is the artist painting, over his shoulder,
the eyes of the statue,
whereupon it is transformed into the god.

Someone wails behind the rusty bars of a window.

That is a convoy of tanks,
an elder fixing shoes under an umbrella,
a boy in a bullock cart with a rag around his head,
a film of smog on the palm leaves,
debris from the bombing of a casino.

This is the artist being led away blindfolded.

A dog fight breaks out in the schoolyard.

That is a souvenir shop,
attended by a girl in a white sarong.

Wisława Szymborska

After every war
someone has to clean up.
Things won't
straighten themselves up, after all.

Someone has to push the rubble
to the side of the road,
so the corpse-filled wagons
can pass.

Someone has to get mired
in scum and ashes,
sofa springs,
splintered glass,
and bloody rags.

Someone has to drag in a girder
to prop up a wall,
Someone has to glaze a window,
rehang a door.

Photogenic it's not,
and takes years.

All the cameras have left
for another war.

We'll need the bridges back,
and new railway stations.
Sleeves will go ragged
from rolling them up.

Someone, broom in hand,
still recalls the way it was.
Someone else listens
and nods with unsevered head.
But already there are those nearby
starting to mill about
who will find it dull.

From out of the bushes
sometimes someone still unearths
rusted-out arguments
and carries them to the garbage pile.

Those who knew
what was going on here

must make way for
those who know little.
And less than little.
And finally as little as nothing.

In the grass that has overgrown
causes and effects,
someone must be stretched out,
blade of grass in his mouth,
gazing at the clouds.

Translated by Joanna Trzeciak

Lawrence Raab

For a long time I was sure
it should be "Jumping Jack Flash," then
the adagio from Schubert's C major Quintet,
but right now I want Oscar Peterson's

"You Look Good to Me." That's my request.
Play it at the end of the service,
after my friends have spoken.
I don't believe I'll be listening in,

but sitting here I'm imagining
you could be feeling what I'd like to feel—
defiance from the Stones, grief
and resignation with Schubert, but now

Peterson and Ray Brown are making
the moment sound like some kind
of release. Sad enough
at first, but doesn't it slide into

tapping your feet, then clapping
your hands, maybe standing up
in that shadowy hall in Paris
in the late sixties when this was recorded,

• • •

getting up and dancing
as I would not have done,
and being dead, cannot, but might
wish for you, who would then

understand what a poem—or perhaps only
the making of a poem, just that moment
when it starts, when so much
is still possible—

has allowed me to feel.
Happy to be there. Carried away.

Virginia Hamilton Adair was a poet and professor, teaching briefly at Wisconsin, William & Mary, and Pomona College, and for many years at California Polytechnic University at Pomona. She published her first book of poetry, *Ants on the Melon*, in 1996, at the age of eighty-three. She died in September 2004.

Kim Addonizio's books of poetry include *Tell Me* (BOA Editions, 2000), which was a finalist for the National Book Award; *Jimmy & Rita* (1997); *The Philosopher's Club* (1994); and *Three West Coast Women*, with Laurie Duesing and Dorianne Laux (1987). She was a founding editor of the journal *Five Fingers Review*. She teaches in the M.F.A. program at Goddard College and lives in San Francisco.

Mark Aiello's work has appeared in *Poetry*, *Northeast*, *Poetry Motel*, *Medicinal Purposes*, *South Coast Poetry Journal*, and, in the U.K., in *Acumen*. Mark lives and works in New York.

Dick Allen has received the Robert Frost Prize for Poetry and the Hart Crane Poetry Prize. His most recent collection is *The Day Before: New Poems* (Sarabande Books, 2003). His poems appear in many of America's leading journals. He recently retired from his position as Charles A. Dana Endowed Chair Professor at the University of Bridgeport.

Yehuda Amichai published eleven volumes of poetry in Hebrew, two novels, and a book of short stories. His work has been translated into thirty-seven languages. He received the Israel Prize for Poetry and was a foreign honorary member of the American Academy of Arts and Letters. He lived in Jerusalem until his death on September 25, 2000.

John Ashbery is the author of over twenty books of poetry. He has received several awards and fellowships, including the Pulitzer Prize for Poetry, the National Book Critics Circle Award, and the National Book Award, all for his collection *Self-Portrait in a Convex Mirror* (1975), as well as the Bollingen Prize and the Ruth Lilly Poetry Prize. He is a former chancellor of the Academy of American Poets and is currently the Charles P. Stevenson, Jr., Professor of Languages and Literature at Bard College.

Margaret Atwood's books have been published in over thirty-five countries. She is the author of more than thirty books of fiction, poetry, and critical essays. Among her numerous honors and awards are a Guggenheim Fellowship, a Molson Award, and a Canada Short Fiction Award. In 1986 *Ms.* magazine named her Woman of the Year. She lives in Toronto.

Julianna Baggott's poetry has appeared and is forthcoming in numerous magazines, including *The Southern Review, Indiana Review, Cream City Review, Green Mountains Review,* and *Spoon River Poetry Review.* Her work has also appeared in *The Best American Poetry* (2000) anthology, edited by Rita Dove. She has also published a novel, *Girl Talk* (2001).

David Baker is the author of six books of poems, most recently *Changeable Thunder,* and two books of criticism. His poems and essays appear in a variety of publications. He serves as poetry editor of *The Kenyon Review* and teaches at Denison University as well as in the M.F.A. program for writers at Warren Wilson College.

Kate Bass lives with her family in Cambridge, England, where she works as an illustrator. She was short-listed for the Arts Council/Radio 4 "First Verse" award in 2002. A short dance based on her first collection, *The Onion House*, was performed in London in January 2003. *The Pasta Maker* is her first full-length collection.

F. J. Bergmann is mostly from Wisconsin, and primarily a failed visual artist who worked with horses in a former life. Her poems have been published in *The North American Review*, *Southern Poetry Review*, and *words & images*, among other publications. In 2003 she received the Rinehart National Poetry Award, and in 2004 won the Pauline Ellis Prose Poem Prize.

Charles Bernstein is the author of *With Strings* (University of Chicago Press, 2001), *Republics of Reality: Poems 1975–1984* (Sun & Moon Press, 2000), *My Way: Speeches and Poems* (Chicago, 1999), and *Content's Dream: Essays 1975–1984* (Northwestern University Press, 2001). He is professor of English at the University of Pennsylvania.

George Bilgere is the author of three collections of poetry, *The Good Kiss* (University of Akron Press), *The Going* (University of Missouri Press), and *Big Bang* (Copper Beech Press). His poems have appeared in several periodicals and anthologies. He is a professor of English at John Carroll University in Cleveland, Ohio.

Laurel Blossom's most recent book of poetry is *Wednesday: New and Selected Poems* (Ridgeway Press, 2004). Her work has also appeared in a number of anthologies and many national journals. She co-founded the writing residency and workshop program The Writers Community, and now serves as chair of the Writers Community Committee of the YMCA National Writer's Voice.

Robert Bly is an award-winning poet, translator, and editor. He started the influential literary magazine for poetry translation in the United States called, successively, *The Fifties*, *The Sixties*, and *The Sev-*

enties, which he recently revived as *The Thousands*. His most recent book of poems is *The Night Abraham Called to the Stars*, which won the Maurice English Award for poetry.

Michelle Boisseau's poetry books include *No Private Life* (1990), *Understory* (1996), and *Trembling Air* (2003). She is also co-author of the college text *Writing Poems*, currently in its sixth edition. Her poems have also appeared in several literary journals. She is a professor at the University of Missouri-Kansas City, where she teaches poetry and poetics.

Jason Bredle earned degrees from Indiana University and the University of Michigan. His chapbook, *A Twelve Step Guide*, won the 2004 DIAGRAM/NMP Chapbook Contest and is available from New Michigan Press. His poems have most recently appeared in *ACM* and *Salt Hill*, and his music reviews in *Resonance*. He lives in Chicago.

Susan Browne's first book, *Buddha's Dogs*, was published in April 2004. Her poems have also appeared in numerous journals. She was selected as the winner of the Four Way Books Intro Prize in Poetry by Edward Hirsch, and she has received awards from the Chester H. Jones Foundation, the National Writers Union, and the Los Angeles Poetry Festival. She lives in Oakland and teaches literature and writing courses at Diablo Valley College in Pleasant Hill, California.

Cathleen Calbert is the author of two books of poetry, *Lessons in Space* (University of Florida Press, 1997) and *Bad Judgment* (Sarabande Books, 1999). Her poetry and fiction have appeared in numerous publications. She has received the "Discovery"/*The Nation* Prize and the Gordon Barber Memorial Award from the Poetry Society of America, among other honors. Currently, she is a professor of English and creative writing at Rhode Island College.

Tom Clark is the author of many volumes of poetry, including *Sleepwalker's Fate*, *Empire of Skin* (Black Sparrow), *White Thought* (Hard

Press/The Figures), and *Night Sky* (Deep Forest), as well as a number of literary biographies, including *Jack Kerouac* (Thunder's Mouth), *Charles Olson: The Allegory of a Poet's Life* (North Atlantic), and *Edward Dorn: A World of Difference* (North Atlantic). Since 1987 he has lectured on poetics as a core faculty member at New College of California.

Suzanne Cleary received the Cecil Hemley Memorial Award from the Poetry Society of America for *Keeping Time* (Carnegie Mellon). Her other honors include awards from *New Letters*, *Mississippi Review*, and the Arvon International Poetry Competition. Her work has appeared in numerous publications. She lives in Peekskill, New York, and is an associate professor of English at SUNY Rockland.

James Cummins has published four collections of poetry, most recently *Then & Now* (Swallow Press, 2004). His poems have appeared in several national journals and have won several awards. Cummins has been curator of the Elliston Poetry Collection at the University of Cincinnati since 1975, where he is also professor of English. He lives in Cincinnati with his wife and two daughters.

Philip Dacey's latest, eighth book is *The Mystery of Max Schmitt: Poems on the Life and Work of Thomas Eakins* (Turning Point Press, 2004). For thirty years a resident of Minnesota, he now lives in Manhattan.

Jim Daniels's latest collection of poems, *Show and Tell: New and Selected Poems*, was published by the University of Wisconsin in 2003. His most recent collection of short fiction, *Detroit Tales*, was published by Michigan State University Press, also in 2003. He teaches at Carnegie Mellon University in Pittsburgh.

Christina Daub co-founded and co-edited *The Plum Review*, an award-winning national poetry journal, and co-founded and co-directs The Plum Writers Retreat annual poets' conference. Her work has appeared most recently in *The Cortland Review*, *The Connecticut Review*, and *Fulcrum*. She teaches at The Writer's Center in

Bethesda, Maryland, in the Maryland Poet-in-the-Schools program, and in Virginia's Pick a Poet program.

Dick Davis is currently a professor of Persian at Ohio State University in Columbus and the author of several books of poetry and translations, including *Touchwood* and *Borrowed Ware*.

Greg Delanty was born in Cork, Ireland, and has lived in America and taught at St. Michael's College in Vermont for over ten years. His earlier books include *Cast in the Fire* (1986), *Southward* (1992), *American Wake* (1995), and, available from OxfordPoets, *The Hellbox* (1998).

Darcie Dennigan was born in Warwick, Rhode Island, in 1975, and began writing poetry while working as a paralegal in Boston. She received an M.F.A. from the University of Michigan and has poems appearing or forthcoming in *Black Warrior Review; Gulf Coast; Forklift, Ohio; jubilat;* and *Salt Hill,* among others. The recipient of a Bread Loaf Writers' Conference scholarship and a Pushcart Prize nomination, she currently resides in Los Angeles.

Carl Dennis is the author of nine books of poetry, including, most recently, *New and Selected Poems, 1974–2004.* His previous book, *Practical Gods,* was awarded the 2002 Pulitzer Prize for Poetry. A recipient of fellowships from the Guggenheim Foundation and the National Endowment for the Arts, he received the Ruth Lilly Poetry Prize from the Modern Poetry Association in 2000. He is artist-in-residence at the State University of New York at Buffalo, and is a member of the faculty of the M.F.A. program in creative writing at Warren Wilson College.

Theodore Deppe is the author of *Children of the Air* (1990) and *The Wanderer King* (1996), both published by Alice James Books, and most recently, *Cape Clear: New & Selected Poems,* published in Ireland by Salmon Publishing in 2002. A recipient of a Pushcart Prize, he has also received a grant from the National Endowment for the Arts. For two decades, he worked as a registered nurse. From 1998 to 1999, he was writer-in-residence at the James Merrill House in Stonington, Connecticut. Currently, he teaches in Lancaster University's distance-learning M.A. program.

W. S. Di Piero was born in South Philadelphia and is the author of numerous volumes of poetry, essays, and translation. His most recent book of poems is *Brother Fire.* He lives in San Francisco, writes a column on the visual arts for the *San Diego Reader,* and teaches part-time at Stanford.

Gregory Djanikian has published four collections of poetry, the most recent of which is *Years Later* (Carnegie Mellon). His new work focuses on the Armenian genocide of 1915 and the Armenian immigrant experience in the United States. He directs the creative writing program at the University of Pennsylvania.

Stephen Dobyns has published ten books of poetry, most recently *Mystery, So Long* (Penguin, 2005), twenty novels, a collection of short stories, and a book of essays. Among his many honors and awards are fellowships from the National Endowment for the Arts and the Guggenheim Foundation. He has taught at a number of colleges and universities, including the University of Iowa and Boston University. He lives in Boston with his wife and three children.

Michael Donaghy was born in the Bronx, New York, in 1954. His collections are *Shibboleth* (1988), which won the Whitbread Prize for Poetry and the Geoffrey Faber Memorial Prize; *Errata* (1993), which received awards from the Arts Council of England and the Ingram Merrill Foundation; and *Conjure* (2002). In 1985, he moved to London, where he worked as a teacher and musician until his untimely death in 2004.

Catherine Doty attended Upsala College and later the University of Iowa where she received an M.F.A. in poetry. Her poems have been widely published. She is the recipient of an Academy of American Poets Prize, fellowships from the New Jersey State Council on the Arts and the New York Foundation for the Arts, and is the recipient of the 2003 Marjorie J. Wilson Award.

Mark Doty is the author of seven books of poems, most recently *School of the Arts* (HarperCollins, 2005), and three volumes of nonfiction prose. His work has received the National Book Critics Circle Award, the T. S. Eliot Prize, a Whiting Writers' Award, and a Lila Wallace–Reader's Digest Writers' Award. He has received fellowships from the Guggenheim Foundation and the National Endowment for the Arts. He lives in New York City and in Houston, where he teaches in the graduate writing program at the University of Houston.

Carol Ann Duffy was born in Glasgow, Scotland, in 1955. She grew up in Stafford, England, and attended the University of Liverpool, where she received an honors degree in 1977. Her poetry publications have received many awards, including both the Forward Prize and the Whitbread Prize for *Mean Time*. She has also written poems for children, including *Meeting Midnight*, published in England. She is a Fellow of the Royal Society of Literature. She currently lives in Manchester, England, where she lectures on poetry for the Writing School at Manchester Metropolitan University.

Stephen Dunn's books of poetry include *Local Visitations* (Norton, 2003); *Different Hours* (Norton, 2000), winner of the 2001 Pulitzer Prize for Poetry; and *New and Selected Poems: 1974–1994* (Norton, 1994). His other honors include the Academy Award for Literature, the James Wright Prize, and fellowships from the National Endowment for the Arts and the New Jersey State Council on the Arts. He is currently Richard Stockton College of New Jersey Distinguished Professor of Creative Writing and lives in Port Republic, New Jersey.

Paul Durcan's most recent collection of poetry is *The Art of Life* (Harvill, 2004). He was poet-in-residence at the Frost Place in 1985, and writer-in-residence at Trinity College, Dublin, in 1990. He has been awarded the Irish American Cultural Institute Poetry Award, the Patrick Kavanagh Award, and the Whitbread Poetry Award. He was joint winner of the 1995 Heinemann Award. He lives in Dublin.

Stuart Dybek, a Guggenheim Fellow and professor of English at Western Michigan University, received a Lannan Literary Award in 1998. He has written a novel-in-stories, *I Sailed with Magellan*; two collections of short stories, *The Coast of Chicago* and *Childhood and Other Neighborhoods*; and a collection of poems, *Brass Knuckles*.

Beth Ann Fennelly, recipient of a 2003 National Endowment for the Arts Award, lives in Oxford, Mississippi, and teaches at Ole Miss. Her first book, *Open House*, won the 2002 Kenyon Review Prize and the 2002 GLCA Award for a First Book. Her second book, *Tender Hooks*, was published by Norton in 2004.

Alice Fulton's most recent book of poems is *Cascade Experiment: Selected Poems* (Norton, 2004). Her other books have won the Rebekah Johnson Bobbitt National Prize for Poetry from the Library of Congress, the National Poetry Series, the Society of Midland Authors Award, and the Associated Writing Programs Award, among others. She has received fellowships from the MacArthur Foundation, the Ingram Merrill Foundation, and the Guggenheim Foundation. She is currently the Ann S. Bowers Professor of English at Cornell University.

Dan Gerber's *Trying to Catch the Horses*, published by Michigan State University Press, received *ForeWord Magazine's* 1999 Gold Medal Book of the Year Award in poetry. He has published five earlier collections of poems, three novels, a collection of short stories, and a book on the Indianapolis 500. He received the Michigan Author Award in 1992 and the Mark Twain Award in 2001. A volume of his selected essays, *A Second Life*, was published in 2001. He and his wife, Debbie, live near Santa Ynez, California, in the only east/west valley in North America.

Douglas Goetsch's poetry collections include *The Job of Being Everybody*, winner of the Cleveland State University Poetry Center Open Competition, *Nobody's Hell* (Hanging Loose Press), and three prize-winning chapbooks. He has received two New York Foundation for the Arts poetry fellowships. He lives in New York City, teaches creative writing to incarcerated teens at Passages Academy, and is founding editor of Jane Street Press.

David Graham is the author of six collections of poems, including *Magic Shows* (1986), *Second Wind* (1990), and *Stutter Monk* (2000). With Kate Sontag, he is co-editor of the essay anthology *After Confession: Poetry as Autobiography* (2001). He was poet-in-residence at the Frost Place in Franconia, New Hampshire, in 1996. He lives in Ripon, Wisconsin, where he is professor of English at Ripon College.

Abigail Gramig's poems have been published in the *Journal of Kentucky Studies*, *Art-Interpres* (Sweden), *Cinco Quetzales* (Guatemala), and others. She has published one book of poems entitled *Dusting the Piano* (Finishing Line Press). She is the artist-in-residence for the Lansing School at Bellarmine University and has received a residency and writer's grant from the Vermont Studio Center. She currently lives in Louisville, Kentucky.

George Green is a native of Grove City, Pennsylvania, and long-time resident of New York City. He earned an M.F.A. degree from The New School and currently teaches poetry and literature at Lehman College, CUNY, in the Bronx.

Debora Greger is the author of seven books of poetry, most recently *Western Art* (Penguin, 2004). She has won, among other honors, the Grolier Prize, the "Discovery" / *The Nation* Prize, the Lavan Younger

Poets Award from the Academy of American Poets, an Award in Literature from the American Academy and Institute of Arts and Letters, and the Brandeis University Award for Poetry. She teaches at the University of Florida and lives in Gainesville, Florida, and in Cambridge, England.

Eamon Grennan is an Irish citizen who has lived in the United States for over thirty years. His most recent collection of poetry, *Still Life with Waterfall*, won the Lenore Marshall Poetry Prize, and his volume of translations, *Leopardi: Selected Poems*, received the PEN Award for Poetry in Translation. He teaches English at Vassar College in Poughkeepsie, New York.

R. S. Gwynn, noted poet, anthologist, and critic, has received the Michael Braude Award from the American Academy of Arts and Letters and the John Gould Fletcher Award for Poetry. His works include *The Area Code of God* (1994) and *No Word of Farewell: New and Selected Poems, 1970–2000* (Story Line Press, 2001). He is also editor of *Poetry: A Pocket Anthology* (Longman, 2004) and *Contemporary American Poetry: A Pocket Anthology* (Longman, 2004). He lives in Beaumont, Texas, where he is professor of English at Lamar University and was honored as the 2004 University Scholar.

Rachel Hadas is the author of twelve books of poetry, essays, and translations. She has received several honors, including a Guggenheim Fellowship in poetry, an Ingram Merrill Foundation grant in poetry, and an award in literature from the American Academy and Institute of Arts and Letters. Her most recent collection of poetry is *Laws* (Zoo Press, 2004). She lives in New York City.

Mark Halliday's four books of poems are *Little Star* (William Morrow, 1987), *Tasker Street* (University of Massachusetts, 1992), *Selfwolf* (University of Chicago, 1999), and *Jab* (University of Chicago, 2002). He has won a Lila Wallace–Reader's Digest Writers' Award, and the Rome Prize. He teaches at Ohio University.

Kerry Hardie's poetry collections include *A Furious Place*, *Cry for the Hot Belly*, and *The Sky Didn't Fall*, all published by Gallery Press. She is the winner of Ireland's National Poetry Prize. Her first novel, *A Winter Marriage*, was published by Little, Brown in 2002, and her second novel is due in 2005. She has been awarded residencies in Ireland, Switzerland, Australia, and China and attended festivals in Paris, Portugal, and Moldova. She lives and works in County Kilkenny, Ireland.

Alison Marsh Harding is a native of Lewiston, Montana, and now lives in Carlsbad, California. Her poems have appeared in *California State Poetry Society*, *Magee Park Poets Anthology*, *Roadspoetry*, *The Poetry Conspiracy*, and *Tidepools*.

Joseph Harrison's poems have appeared in, among other places, *The Best American Poetry* (1998) anthology, *The Antioch Review*, *Boston Review*, *The Kenyon Review*, *The Paris Review*, *Parnassus*, and *The Yale Review*. *Someone Else's Name* was published by Waywiser Press in the UK in 2003, and by Zoo Press the following year. He lives in Baltimore.

Anthony Hecht published eight books of poetry, including *The Darkness and the Light* (Knopf, 2001) and *The Hard Hours* (1967), which won the Pulitzer Prize. He was also an essayist, translator, and editor. He received the Bollingen Prize, the Ruth Lilly Poetry Prize, and the Harriet Monroe Poetry Award, and fellowships from the Academy of American Poets, the Ford Foundation, the Guggenheim Foundation, and the Rockefeller Foundation. He was a Chancellor Emeritus of the Academy of American Poets and lived in Washington, D.C. He died on October 20, 2004.

Bob Hicok's fourth collection of poetry is *Insomnia Diary* (Pitt, 2004). *Animal Soul* was a finalist for the National Book Critics Circle Award. He lives, teaches, and walks his dog in Blacksburg, Virginia.

Edward Hirsch has published six books of poems, most recently *Lay Back the Darkness* (Knopf, 2004). He has also written three prose books, including *How to Read a Poem and Fall in Love with Poetry* (1999), a national bestseller. He has received a Guggenheim Fellowship, an American Academy of Arts and Letters Award for Literature, and a MacArthur Fellowship. He is currently the president of the John Simon Guggenheim Memorial Foundation.

Ben Howard is the author of six books, most recently *Dark Pool* (Salmon Publishing, Ireland, 2004). For the past three decades he has contributed poems, essays, and reviews to literary journals here and abroad, and he has received numerous awards. He teaches literature, writing, classical guitar, and Buddhist meditation at Alfred University.

Christopher Howell has published eight collections of poems, most recently *Light's Ladder,* from the University of Washington Press. His poems, translations, and essays have been frequently and widely published in anthologies and journals. He teaches at Eastern Washington University's Inland NW Center for Writers, where he is also senior editor for the EWU Press. He lives in Spokane with his family.

Bruce A. Jacobs is the author of the poetry collection *Speaking Through My Skin,* which won the Naomi Long Madgett Poetry Award, and the nonfiction book *Race Manners: Navigating the Minefield Between Black and White Americans*. His work has appeared in several journals and anthologies. He has had writing residencies at the MacDowell Colony and elsewhere. He lives in Baltimore.

Donald Justice was born in Miami, Florida, in 1925. He was the author of many books and the recipient of many grants and prizes, including the Pulitzer Prize for his *Selected Poems* in 1979, and the Bollingen Prize. He taught at a number of universities, chiefly the University of Iowa and the University of Florida. He died in August 2004, shortly before the publication of his *Collected Poems*.

Katia Kapovich is a bilingual poet writing in English and Russian. Her Russian verse has received wide acclaim in her country of origin.

Her English-language poems have appeared in *The London Review of Books, Jacket, Ploughshares, Harvard Review, The Dark Horse,* and numerous other journals. In 2001, the U.S. Library of Congress awarded her its Witter Bynner Poetry Fellowship. She co-edits *Fulcrum: an annual of poetry and aesthetics* and lives in Cambridge, Massachusetts.

Kirsten Kaschock's first book, *Unfathoms,* was published by Slope Editions in 2004. Her poetic work has appeared in journals including *The Iowa Review, Indiana Review, Hayden's Ferry Review,* and *American Letters & Commentary.* An associate editor of *Verse,* she lives in Suwanee, Georgia, with her husband and two children.

Jane Kenyon published five collections of poetry: *From Room to Room, The Boat of Quiet Hours, Let Evening Come, Constance,* and *Otherwise: New & Selected Poems,* and translated the poems of Anna Akhmatova. In 1994 she was diagnosed with leukemia; she died in 1995.

David Kirby is the Robert O. Lawton Distinguished Professor of English at Florida State University. A recipient of Guggenheim and National Endowment for the Arts fellowships, he is the author of, most recently, *The Ha-Ha,* which was chosen by Dave Smith for Louisiana State University's Southern Messenger Poets series. He is married to the poet Barbara Hamby.

Bill Knott is the author of ten previous volumes of poetry, including his groundbreaking first book, *The Naomi Poems* (1968), and *Laugh at the End of the World: Collected Comic Poems 1969–1999.* He is an associate professor at Emerson College.

Kenneth Koch wrote several volumes of poetry, most recently *A Possible World, Sun Out, New Addresses,* and *Straits,* published by Knopf. He was also a playwright and essayist. He won the Bollingen Prize (1995) and the Bobbitt Library of Congress Poetry Prize (1996), was a finalist for the National Book Award (2000), and received the Phi

Beta Kappa Award for Poetry (2001). He taught at Columbia University. He died in July 2002.

Ron Koertge lives in South Pasadena, California. He is the recipient of grants from the National Endowment for the Arts and the California Arts Council. His poems have appeared in too many anthologies to mention. His recent books of poems include *Geography of the Forehead* from the University of Arkansas Press, and *Fever*, from Red Hen Press. He is also the author of a dozen prizewinning novels for young adults, the most recent being *Boy Girl Boy* from Harcourt. He may be seen at many racetracks, squandering his savings.

Ted Kooser, a retired vice president of Lincoln Benefit Life, an insurance company in Nebraska, is the author of ten books, including *Delights and Shadows* (Copper Canyon, 2004) and *Sure Signs: New and Selected Poems* (University of Pittsburgh, 1980). He has won two fellowships from the National Endowment for the Arts, a Pushcart Prize, the James Boatwright Prize from *Shenandoah*, a Merit Award from the Nebraska Arts Council, a Nebraska Book Award for Poetry, and many other prizes. He was named U.S. Poet Laureate in 2004.

Laurie Lamon is associate professor of English at Whitworth College in Spokane, Washington. Her poems have appeared in magazines and journals, including *The Atlantic Monthly*, *Ploughshares*, *The Colorado Review*, *Arts & Letters*, *Journal of Contemporary Culture*, and *The New Republic*. She was awarded a Pushcart Prize in 2001, and her work has been included on the Poetry Daily website. Her first collection, *The Fork Without Hunger*, is forthcoming from CavanKerry Press. She lives with her husband, William Siems, and their two Scottish terriers.

Li-Young Lee is the author of *Books of My Nights* (2001); *The City in Which I Love You* (1991); and *Rose* (1986), which won the Delmore

Schwartz Memorial Poetry Award. He has also written a memoir entitled *The Winged Seed: A Remembrance* (1995), which received an American Book Award from the Before Columbus Foundation. He lives in Chicago with his wife, Donna, and their two sons.

David Lehman's books of poetry include *The Daily Mirror*, *The Evening Sun*, and *When a Woman Loves a Man*. He is the series editor of *The Best American Poetry*, the anthology series he established in 1988.

Margaret Levine's poems have appeared in *The Quarterly* and *Open City*, and most recently on the Poetry 180 website. She was born in Canada and now lives in Phoenix, Arizona.

Michael Longley was born in Belfast in 1939 and educated at the Royal Belfast Academical Institution. His most recent collection of poetry is *Snow Water* (Cape, 2004). He has been awarded the Queen's Gold Medal for Poetry, the Whitbread Poetry Prize, the Hawthornden Prize, the T. S. Eliot Prize, and the Belfast Arts Award for Literature. He is editor of *20th Century Irish Poems* (2002). He lives in Belfast with his wife, the critic Edna Longley.

Daniel Lusk's most recent book is *Kissing the Ground: New and Selected Poems*. He teaches at the University of Vermont.

Thomas Lux holds the Bourne Chair in Poetry and is the director of the McEver Visiting Writers Program at the Georgia Institute of Technology. He has been awarded three National Endowment for the Arts grants and the Kingsley Tufts Award and is a former Guggenheim Fellow. His most recent collection of poetry is *The Cradle Place*. He lives in Atlanta.

Norman MacCaig, a Scottish poet, published sixteen collections of poetry. His work is known for its humor, simplicity of language, and great popularity. He was awarded the Society of Authors Award, the

Heinemann Award, the Poetry Society Award, and the Queen's Medal for Poetry. He died in 1996 at the age of eighty-five.

Elizabeth Macklin is the author of two books of poetry, most recently *You've Just Been Told* (Norton, 2000). Her poems, essays, and translations have appeared in *The Nation, The New Yorker, The Paris Review, The Yale Review,* and elsewhere. She has been awarded an Ingram Merrill Foundation poetry prize, a Guggenheim Fellowship, and the Amy Lowell Poetry Traveling Scholarship, which she spent studying Basque in Spain's Basque country. She lives in New York City.

Gary Margolis is director of counseling and associate professor of English at Middlebury College in Vermont. He has been a Robert Frost Fellow at the Bread Loaf Writers' Conference and recipient of a Vermont Council on the Arts award and a Millay Colony residency. His most recent collection, *Fire in the Orchard,* was published by Autumn House Press. He lives with his wife in Cornwall, Vermont, where he is a volunteer firefighter.

Cate Marvin received her B.A. from Marlboro College in Vermont, and holds two M.F.A. degrees: one from the University of Houston (poetry), and the other from Iowa Writers' Workshop (fiction). She has been awarded scholarships to attend both Bread Loaf and Sewanee Writers' Conferences. Her collection of poetry, *World's Tallest Disaster,* received the Kathryn A. Morton Prize in Poetry, the Greenwall Fund Grant from the Academy of American Poets, and the Kate Tufts Discovery Award.

Donna Masini is the author of *Turning to Fiction* (Norton, 2004), *That Kind of Danger,* selected by Mona Van Duyn for the Barnard Women Poets Prize, and *About Yvonne,* a novel. Her poems have appeared in *The American Poetry Review, TriQuarterly, The Paris Review, The Georgia Review, Parnassus, Open City, Boulevard, Lyric,* and other publications. She was a recipient of a National Endowment for the

Arts fellowship and a Pushcart Prize. She teaches at Hunter College and lives in New York City.

William Matthews published eleven books of poetry, including *Time & Money* (1996), which won the National Book Critics Circle Award, and a book of essays entitled *Curiosities* (1989). He served as president of Associated Writing Programs and of the Poetry Society of America, and as a member and chair of the Literature Panel of the National Endowment for the Arts. He received fellowships from the Guggenheim and Ingram Merrill foundations, and he was awarded the Ruth Lilly Poetry Prize. He died of a heart attack on November 12, 1997, the day after his fifty-fifth birthday.

Glyn Maxwell has published several books of poetry, most recently *The Nerve* (Mariner, 2004). Among the honors he has received are the Somerset Maugham Prize and the E. M. Forster Prize, which he was awarded in 1997 by the American Academy of Arts and Letters. He was appointed poetry editor at *The New Republic* in 2001, and is a Fellow of the Royal Society of Literature. He now lives with his wife and their daughter in New York and teaches at Princeton University.

Don McKay has published nine books of poetry, including *Birding, Or Desire* (1983), *Sanding Down This Rocking Chair on a Windy Night* (1987), *Night Field* (1991), *Apparatus* (1997), and *Another Gravity* (2000). He is also known as a poetry editor, and he has taught poetry in universities across the country. He currently lives in British Columbia.

Lynne McMahon's most recent book, *Sentimental Standards*, was published by David Godine in October 2003. Her previous books include *The House of Entertaining Science*, *Devolution of the Nude*, and *Faith*. She has received the Ingram Merrill Foundation Award and a Guggenheim Foundation grant. She received the 2003 Award in Literature from the Academy of Arts and Letters. She lives in Columbia, Missouri, with her husband, Sherod Santos, and their two sons.

Philip Memmer is the author of the poetry collection *Sweetheart, Baby, Darling* (Word Press, 2004). His poems have appeared widely in journals, including *Poetry*, *Poetry Northwest*, and *Tar River Poetry*. He lives in upstate New York.

W. S. Merwin is the author of many books of poems, prose, and translations. He has been the recipient of many awards and prizes, including the Fellowship of the Academy of American Poets (of which he is now a Chancellor), the Pulitzer Prize for Poetry, and the Bollingen Prize. Most recently he has received the Tanning Prize for mastery in the art of poetry, a Lila Wallace–Reader's Digest Writers' Award, and the Ruth Lilly Poetry Prize.

Czeslaw Milosz was awarded the Nobel Prize for Literature in 1980. He wrote virtually all of his poems in his native Polish, although his work was banned in Poland until after he won the Nobel Prize. He also translated the works of other Polish writers into English, and co-translated his own works with such poets as Robert Hass and Robert Pinsky. He died on August 14, 2004.

Robert Minhinnick has published eight volumes of poetry and essays, and also translations from the Welsh. His most recent books are a collection of poems, *After the Hurricane* (Carcanet, 2002), and a book of translations, *The Adulterer's Tongue* (Carcanet, 2003). He won the Forward Prize for Best Poem in 1999 and 2003. He currently edits the international quarterly *Poetry Wales.*

Frederick Morgan was the author of more than a dozen books of poetry and was a founder and, for fifty-five years, the editor of *The Hudson Review*, one of the nation's most prestigious literary journals. He died in February 2004.

Robert Morgan, poet and fiction writer, is the author of twenty-four books, including *The Mountains Won't Remember Us*, *The Strange Attractor*, and the Oprah selection *Gap Creek*. He teaches at Cornell University.

Paul Muldoon has published over ten books of poetry. A Fellow of the Royal Society of Literature and the American Academy of Arts and Sciences, he has won the T. S. Eliot Prize, an American Academy of Arts and Letters Award in Literature, the Pulitzer Prize for Poetry, and the Shakespeare Prize. *The Times Literary Supplement* called Muldoon "the most significant English-language poet born since the Second World War."

Erin Murphy is the author of *Science of Desire* (Word Press) and *Too Much of This World* (Mammoth Books), winner of the Anthony Piccione Poetry Prize. She teaches literature and creative writing at Washington College in Maryland.

Carol Muske-Dukes is the founder and director of the graduate program in literature and creative writing at the University of Southern California. Her last collection of poetry, *Sparrow*, was nominated for the National Book Award. She has been the recipient of many awards, among them a Guggenheim fellowship, and has written three novels and a collection of essays, *Married to the Icepick Killer*. She lives in Los Angeles with her daughter.

Jack Myers, 2003 Texas Poet Laureate, is the author of seventeen books of and about poetry, most recently the textbook *The Poet's Portable Workshop* (Heinle). His awards include the National Poetry Series, two Texas Institute of Letters awards, The Violet Crown Award, and two National Endowment for the Arts fellowships. He teaches creative writing at Southern Methodist University in Dallas.

Aimee Nezhukumatathil is the author of *Miracle Fruit* (Tupelo Press, 2003), winner of the *ForeWord Magazine* Book of the Year

Award in Poetry and a finalist for the Glasgow Prize and the Asian-American Literary Award. She is assistant professor of English at the State University of New York at Fredonia. She lives with her dog, Villanelle (www.aimeenez.com).

Philip Nikolayev's collection of poems is *Monkey Time* (Verse Press, 2003), which won the 2001 Verse Prize. His poems have also appeared in such journals as *The Paris Review, Grand Street, Verse, Stand, Jacket*, and many others across the English-speaking world. He co-edits *Fulcrum: an annual of poetry and aesthetics*. He lives in Cambridge, Massachusetts, with his wife, the poet Katia Kapovich, and their daughter, Sophia.

Edward Nobles has published two books of poetry, *Through One Tear* and *The Bluestone Walk*. His poems have appeared in numerous magazines, including *The Gettysburg Review, The Kenyon Review, The Paris Review*, and *Tin House*. He lives in Bangor, Maine, where is risk manager for the University of Maine System.

Naomi Shihab Nye has won wide praise for her work as a poet, teacher, essayist, and anthologist. Her books include *Words Under Words: Selected Poems* and *19 Varieties of Gazelle: Poems of the Middle East*. She lives with her family in San Antonio, Texas.

Sharon Olds was born in San Francisco and educated at Stanford and Columbia. She was the New York State Poet Laureate from 1998 to 2000. She teaches poetry workshops in the Graduate Creative Writing Program at New York University and was one of the founders of the NYU workshop program at Goldwater Hospital on Roosevelt Island in New York City. Her most recent book is *Strike Sparks: Selected Poems, 1980–2002* (Knopf, 2004). Her work has received the Harriet Monroe Prize, the National Book Critics Circle Award, and the Lamont Selection of the Academy of American Poets. She lives in New York City.

Leanne O'Sullivan is an arts student at University College Cork, Ireland. She has been writing poetry since she was twelve, and her first book, *Waiting for My Clothes*, was published by Bloodaxe in 2004. She won the RTE Rattlebag Poetry Slam (2002) and the Seacat Irish National Poetry Competition (Secondary School division, 2001).

Ron Padgett's books include a collection of poems, *You Never Know*, and a memoir, *Oklahoma Tough: My Father, King of the Tulsa Bootleggers*. He is the editor of *The Handbook of Poetic Forms* and the translator of Blaise Cendrars's *Complete Poems*. Padgett has taught imaginative writing at Columbia University and Brooklyn College, and for twenty years he was publications director of Teachers & Writers Collaborative. His poetry has received awards from the American Academy of Arts and Letters and the Guggenheim Foundation. His new book, from Coffee House Press, is *Joe: A Memoir of Joe Brainard*.

Alan Michael Parker is the author of three books of poems, including *Love Song with Motor Vehicles* (BOA Editions, 2003), and a novel, *Cry Uncle* (University of Mississippi Press, 2005), and co-editor of two reference works on poets and poetry. His essays and reviews have appeared in *The New Yorker*, *The New York Times Book Review*, and *Salon*. He teaches at Davidson College, where he directs the program in creative writing, and at Queens University. For more information, visit, www.amparker.com.

Linda Pastan is the author of eleven books, most recently *The Last Uncle*. She was Poet Laureate of Maryland for four years and received the Ruth Lilly Poetry Prize in 2003.

Ricardo Pau-Llosa is a poet and art critic who lives in Miami. He has published five collections of poetry, the last three from Carnegie Mellon University Press: *Cuba* (1993), *Vereda Tropical* (1999), and *The Mastery Impulse* (2003). As an art critic and curator he specializes in modern and contemporary Latin American art.

Peter Pereira divides his time between work as a family physician at High Point Community Clinic in West Seattle, and volunteering as an editor at Floating Bridge Press. Winner of the 1997 "Discovery"/ *The Nation* Prize, his books include *The Lost Twin* (Grey Spider Press, 2000) and *Saying the World* (Copper Canyon, 2003), which won the Hayden Carruth Award and was a finalist for the Lambda Literary Award, the Triangle Publishing Award, and the PEN/USA Award in Poetry.

Lucia Perillo has published four poetry collections: *The Oldest Map with the Name America*; *The Body Mutinies*, for which she won the PEN/Revson Foundation Poetry fellowship and several other awards; *Dangerous Life*, which received the Norma Farber Award from the Poetry Society of America; and, most recently, *Luck Is Luck*. A 2000 MacArthur fellow, her poems have appeared in such magazines as *The New Yorker*, *The Atlantic*, and *The Kenyon Review*, and they have been included in the Pushcart and *The Best American Poetry* anthologies.

Mark Perlberg is the author of three books of poems: *The Burning Field* (Morrow), *The Feel of the Sun* (Ohio University Press), and *The Impossible Toystore* (Louisiana State University Press). He is a founder and now director emeritus of The Poetry Center of Chicago. He lives with his wife in Chicago.

Lynn Powell is the author of *The Zones of Paradise* (2003) and *Old & New Testaments* (1995), which won the Brittingham Prize in Poetry and the Great Lakes Colleges Association's New Writers Award. Her work has been anthologized in collections such as *Cornbread Nation: The Best of Southern Food Writing* (2002), *Her Words: Diverse Voices in Contemporary Appalachian Women's Poetry* (2002), and *O Taste & See: Food Poems* (2003). A native of East Tennessee, she lives and teaches in Oberlin, Ohio.

Lawrence Raab's most recent book of poetry is *Visible Signs: New and Selected Poems* (Penguin, 2003). His poems have appeared in such magazines as *Poetry*, *The New Yorker*, *The Paris Review*, and *The Nation*. He is professor of English at Williams College in Williamstown, Massachusetts.

Victoria Redel is the author of two poetry books, *Swoon* and *Already the World*. She is also the author of the novel *Loverboy* (Harcourt) and a collection of short fiction, *Where the Road Bottoms Out* (Knopf). She has received the Tom and Stan Wick Poetry Prize, the S. Mariella Gable Award, a National Endowment for the Arts fellowship, and a fellowship from the Fine Arts Work Center in Provincetown. She lives in New York City and is currently on the faculty of Sarah Lawrence College and Columbia University.

Oliver Rice has received the Theodore Roethke Prize, has been nominated for a Pushcart Prize, and was twice featured on Poetry Daily. His work appears in *Ohio Review*'s anthology *New and Selected* and in Bedford/St. Martin's college textbooks *Poetry: An Introduction* and *The Bedford Introduction to Literature*.

Yannis Ritsos, born in 1909, was one of Greece's most prolific, distinguished, and celebrated poets whose many honors included the Alfred de Vigny Award (1975) and the Lenin Prize (1977). Ritsos died in 1990.

Robin Robertson's *A Painted Field* won a number of awards for first publication in the U.K., including the 1997 Forward Prize for Best First Collection and the Scottish First Book of the Year Award. A second collection, *Slow Air*, appeared from Harcourt in 2003. In 2004 he received the E. M. Forster Award from the American Academy of Arts and Letters.

Pattiann Rogers has published nine books of poetry, a book-length essay, *The Dream of the Marsh Wren*, and *A Covenant of Seasons*, poems and monotypes, in collaboration with the artist Joellyn Duesberry. She is the recipient of two National Endowment for the Arts grants, a Guggenheim Fellowship, and a Poetry Fellowship from the Lannan Foundation. Her poems have won the Tietjens Prize, the Hokin Prize, and the Bock Prize from *Poetry* as well as five Pushcart Prizes, among other awards. She is the mother of two sons and two grandsons and lives with her husband, a retired geophysicist, in Colorado.

Aidan Rooney-Céspedes is an Irish poet living in Hingham, Massachusetts. In 1996 he was winner of the W. B. Yeats Poetry Competition and in 1997 he received the *Sunday Tribune*/Hennessy Cognac Award for New Irish Poetry. He has been published widely in journals in Europe and North America, most recently or forthcoming in *The Irish Times, TriQuarterly, Poetry Review, Harvard Review,* and *Metre.* His first collection of poems—*Day Release*—appeared from the Gallery Press in 2000.

J. Allyn Rosser's first book, *Bright Moves* (Northeastern University Press, 1990), won the Morse Poetry Prize. She has been the recipient of a grant from the National Endowment for the Arts, a Pushcart Prize, the Lavan Award from the Academy of American Poets, and several other awards. She has taught at the Universities of Houston and Michigan, and now lives in Athens, Ohio, where she teaches in the creative writing program at Ohio University.

Joey Roth was editor of the literary magazine at Montclair High School in Montclair, N.J. His first poem was published in the high school writing section of *Hanging Loose Magazine.* Now in college, he is concentrating on short fiction.

Jane Routh is a photographer who manages woodlands and a flock of geese in North Lancashire. *Circumnavigation* is her first collection. It won the Poetry Business Book & Pamphlet Competition, and was short-listed for the Forward Prize in 2003.

Kay Ryan has published five collections of poetry, including *Say Uncle* (Grove Press, 2000); *Elephant Rocks* (1996); *Flamingo Watching* (1994), which was a finalist for both the Lamont Poetry Selection and the Lenore Marshall Prize; *Strangely Marked Metal* (1985); and *Dragon Acts to Dragon Ends* (1983). Her work has been published in a variety of publications. She lives in the San Francisco Bay area.

Mary Jo Salter is the author of five collections of poetry and a children's book, *The Moon Comes Home*. Her awards include fellowships from the Ingram Merrill and Guggenheim Foundations. A vice president of the Poetry Society of America, she is also a co-editor of *The Norton Anthology of Poetry*. She is the Emily Dickinson Senior Lecturer in the Humanities at Mount Holyoke College and lives with her family in Amherst, Massachusetts.

May Sarton was an American poet and novelist. Her first collection of lyrics, *Encounter in April* (1937), was followed by numerous volumes of poetry. In addition to her many novels, Sarton wrote such personal works as *The Hours by the Sea* (1977) and *After the Stroke: A Journal* (1988). A professor at both Harvard University and Wellesley College, she died in 1995 at the age of eighty-three.

Vijay Seshadri is the author of *Wild Kingdom*. His poems have appeared in *The New Yorker*, *The Paris Review*, and *The Best American Poetry*. He was born in India and currently lives in Brooklyn, New York.

Harvey Shapiro's many books include *How Charlie Shavers Died and Other Poems* (Wesleyan, 2001), *National Cold Storage Company* (Wesleyan, 1988), and *Battle Report* (Wesleyan, 1966). He has edited both *The New York Times Book Review* and *The New York Times Magazine*.

Robert Shaw is a professor of English at Mount Holyoke College. His books of poetry include *The Post Office Murals Restored* and *Below the Surface*.

Julie Sheehan's first book, *Thaw* (Fordham, 2001), won the Poets Out Loud Prize and appeared with an introduction by Marie Ponsot. The 2003 recipient of *The Paris Review*'s Bernard F. Conners Prize for Poetry, Sheehan has also published poems in *The Yale Review, Pleiades, Raritan, Salmagundi, Southwest Review,* and *The Kenyon Review,* among others.

Charles Simic is one of America's leading poets, as well as an essayist and translator. His 1990 collection, *The World Doesn't End: Prose Poems,* was awarded the Pulitzer Prize, and he has received numerous other literary honors. Born in Belgrade, Simic now lives in New Hampshire, where he teaches American literature and creative writing at the University of New Hampshire.

Louis Simpson has published over seventeen books of original poetry, including *The Owner of the House: New Collected Poems, 1940–2001* (BOA Editions, 2003). He is also the author of several books of literary criticism, translations, and a memoir. Among his many honors are the Prix de Rome, fellowships from the Guggenheim Foundation, and the Columbia Medal for Excellence. He lives in Setauket, New York.

William Stafford published over sixty books of poetry and prose, including *Traveling through the Dark,* which won the National Book Award in 1963. He taught at Lewis & Clark College for over thirty years, and died at his home in Lake Oswego, Oregon, on August 28, 1993.

Timothy Steele is professor of English at California State University, Los Angeles. He is the author of *Missing Measures: Modern Poetry and the Revolt Against Meter* and *All the Fun's in How You Say a Thing: An Explanation of Meter and Versification.* His collections of poetry include *The Color Wheel* and *Sapphics and Uncertainties: Poems 1970–1986.*

Kevin Stein, Illinois Poet Laureate, is the author of seven books of poetry and literary criticism, including the collection *American Ghost Roses* (University of Illinois Press, 2005). Stein's poems and essays have appeared widely in journals. Among his honors are the Frederick Bock Prize awarded by *Poetry* and the *Indiana Review* Prize. He is currently Caterpillar Professor of English at Bradley University.

Gerald Stern is the author of thirteen books of poetry including *This Time: New and Selected Poems* (Norton, 1998), which won the National Book Award. He has also published a collection of personal essays, *What I Can't Bear Losing: Notes from a Life* (Norton, 2003). He has taught at many universities, and for fifteen years was senior poet at the Iowa Writers' Workshop. His several awards include a Guggenheim Fellowship, three National Endowment for the Arts fellowships, the Lamont Poetry Prize, and the Ruth Lilly Poetry Prize. He was the first Poet Laureate of New Jersey, serving from 2000 to 2002.

Paul Suntup was born in South Africa. He is currently co-director of the Tebot Bach monthly reading series in Huntington Beach, California, and is editor of *So Luminous the Wildflowers: An Anthology of California Poets* (Tebot Bach, 2003). His work has appeared in numerous publications including *Spillway, Beyond The Valley of The Contemporary Poets Anthology, Artlife* and *Rattle*.

Joyce Sutphen is the author of three books of poetry, most recently *Naming the Stars* (Holy Cow! Press, 2004). Her poems have also appeared in many journals, including *Poetry, Hayden's Ferry,* and *The Gettysburg Review*. Her awards include a Loft-McKnight Award in Poetry, the Eunice Tietjen's Memorial Award (*Poetry*), a Minnesota State Arts Board Fellowship, a Salzburg Fellowship, and Travel and Study awards from the Jerome Foundation.

Wisława Szymborska has published more than fifteen books of poetry. Her poems have been translated into many languages; her collections available in English include *Miracle Fair: Selected Poems of Wisława Szymborska* (Norton, 2001) and *View with a Grain of Sand: Selected Poems* (1995). Among her many honors and awards are a Goethe Prize, a Herder Prize, and a Polish PEN Club prize. She won the Nobel Prize for Literature in 1996. She has lived in Krakow since 1931.

James Tate's *Selected Poems* was published in 1991, for which he received the Pulitzer Prize and the William Carlos Williams Award. His volume of poems *Worshipful Company of Fletchers* (1994) was awarded the National Book Award. In 1995, the American Academy of Poets presented him with the Wallace Stevens Prize. His latest book is *Return to the City of White Donkeys.* He teaches at the University of Massachusetts.

Diane Thiel is the author of four books of poetry and nonfiction, most recently *Resistance Fantasies: Poems* (Story Line Press, 2004). She has also written two creative writing textbooks, both published by Longman in 2004. Her work appears in numerous publications, including *Poetry, The Hudson Review,* and *The Best American Poetry* (1999). Her work has received numerous awards, including the Robert Frost Award, the Robinson Jeffers Award, and the New Millennium Writings Award. She is currently an assistant professor of English/Creative Writing at the University of New Mexico.

Tony Towle's latest major publication is *The History of the Invitation: New & Selected Poems 1963–2000* (Hanging Loose Press), his eleventh book of poetry. He has also authored *Memoir 1960–1963* (Faux Press) about being a young poet in New York in the early '60s. He received the Frank O'Hara Award in 1970, and fellowships from the National Endowment for the Arts and the New York State Council on the Arts, among other honors.

Paul Violi is the author of ten books of poetry, including *Breakers*, a selection of long poems from Coffee House Press, and *Fraca, The Curious Builder*, and *Likewise* from Hanging Loose Press. In 2001 he received the Zabel Award from the American Academy of Arts and Letters. He is also the recipient of the John Ciardi Lifetime Achievement Award and two poetry fellowships from the National Endowment for the Arts. He teaches imaginative writing at Columbia University as well as courses at New York University and in the graduate writing program at New School University. He lives in Putnam Valley, New York.

Diane Wald has been publishing in literary magazines since 1966, and has received grants from the Fine Arts Work Center in Provincetown and the Massachusetts Council on the Arts. Her most recent book is *The Yellow Hotel* (Verse Press, 2002). She has received the Grolier Poetry Prize, the Denny Award, the Open Voice Award, and the Green Lake Chapbook Award. She lives outside of Boston with her husband and works for animal welfare at the Massachusetts Society for the Prevention of Cruelty to Animals.

Tom Wayman's recent books include *My Father's Cup*, a collection of his poems, and *The Dominion of Love*, an anthology of contemporary Canadian love poems. He teaches at the University of Calgary, Alberta.

Rebecca Wee is a professor of creative writing at Augustana College in Illinois. She has received several awards for her poetry. She has served as the editor for *The Minnesota Review* and as editorial assistant to Carolyn Forché on her 1993 anthology *Against Forgetting: Twentieth-Century Poetry of Witness*.

C. K. Williams is the author of numerous books of poetry, including *The Singing* (Farrar, Straus and Giroux, 2003); *Repair* (1999), which won the 2000 Pulitzer Prize; and *Flesh and Blood* (1987), which won the National Book Critics Circle Award. He has also published five works of translation. Among his many awards and honors are an American Academy of Arts and Letters Award, a Guggenheim Fellowship, the Lila Wallace–Reader's Digest Writers' Award, the PEN/Voelcker Award for Poetry, and a Pushcart Prize. He teaches in the creative writing program at Princeton University and lives part of each year in Paris.

Hugo Williams was born in 1942. He has published ten books of poetry as well as two travel books. His column "Freelance" appears regularly in *The Times Literary Supplement*, and his last book, *Billy's Rain* (1999), won the T. S. Eliot prize. A recipient of the Queens Gold Medal in 2004, he currently lives in London.

Cecilia Woloch is the director of Summer Poetry in Idyllwild and a member of the M.F.A. in creative writing faculty at New England College. She has conducted poetry workshops in venues and institutions throughout the United States and Europe, ranging from public schools and universities to prisons and hospitals. In 2003 she launched a poetry outreach program in conjunction with the Georgia Institute of Technology and Communities in Schools of Atlanta. She has homes in both Los Angeles and Atlanta.

Franz Wright's seventh full-length collection of poems, *Walking to Martha's Vineyard* (Knopf, 2003), received the 2004 Pulitzer Prize for Poetry. He lives in Waltham, Massachusetts, with his wife, Elizabeth.

Robert Wrigley teaches in the creative writing program at the University of Idaho. A former Guggenheim and two-time National Endowment for the Arts fellow, he has published six books of poetry, including his most recent, *Lives of the Animals* (2003). He lives in the woods near Moscow, Idaho, with his wife, the writer Kim Barnes, and their children.

Dean Young has published five books of poems, most recently *Elegy on Toy Piano* (University of Pittsburgh Press, 2005). He has received a Stegner fellowship from Stanford, two fellowships from the National Endowment for the Arts, and a Guggenheim Fellowship. His poems have appeared three times in *The Best American Poetry* series. He is on the permanent faculty of the Iowa Writers' Workshop and also teaches in the Warren Wilson low-residency M.F.A. program. He splits his time between Iowa City and Berkeley, California, where he lives with his wife, the novelist Cornelia Nixon.

Kevin Young is the author of three previous collections of poetry and the Library of America's *John Berryman: Selected Poems*; Everyman's Library Pocket Poets anthology *Blue Poems*; and *Giant Steps: The New Generation of African American Writers*. His most recent book, *Jelly Roll*, was a finalist for the National Book Award and the *Los Angeles Times* Book Prize. Young is currently Ruth Lilly Professor of Poetry at Indiana University.

Adam Zagajewski is one of Poland's most famous contemporary poets as well as a novelist and essayist. His work has been translated into many languages. His most recent book in English is *Mysticism for Beginners* (Farrar, Straus & Giroux, 1997). Among his honors and awards are a fellowship from the Berliner Kunstlerprogramm and a Prix de la Liberté. Since 1988, he has served as visiting associate professor of English in the Creative Writing Program at the University of Houston. He lives in Paris and Houston.

index of contributors

index of titles

permission credits

Grateful acknowledgment is made to the following to reprint previously
published material:

Mark Aiello: "Chapter One" by Mark Aiello originally published in *Poetry*,
vol. CLXXXII, no. 6, September 2003, copyright © 2003 by Mark Aiello.
Reprinted by permission of the author.

Anvil Press Poetry: "Valentine" from *Mean Time* by Carol Ann Duffy, published by
Anvil Press Poetry in 1993. Reprinted by permission of Anvil Press Poetry.

Autumn House Press and Gary Margolis: "A Shadow of a Nest" from *Fire in the
Orchard* by Gary Margolis, copyright © 2002 by Gary Margolis. Reprinted by
permission of the author and Autumn House Press.

F. J. Bergmann: "An Apology" by F. J. Bergmann originally published in *North
American Review*, March–April 2003, copyright © 2003 by F. J. Bergmann.
Reprinted by permission of the author.

Charles Bernstein: "Warrant" by Charles Bernstein, copyright © Charles
Bernstein. Reprinted by permission of the author.

Bloodaxe Books: "Crescendo" and "Waiting for My Clothes" from *Waiting for My
Clothes* by Leanne O'Sullivan (Bloodaxe Books, 2004). Reprinted by
permission of Bloodaxe Books.

Laurel Blossom: "Fight" by Laurel Blossom, copyright © 1993 by Laurel
Blossom. Reprinted by permission of the author.

BOA Editions, Ltd.: "Slow Children at Play" and "The Hammock" from *Late*
by Cecilia Woloch, copyright © 2003 by Cecilia Woloch; "From Blossoms"

from *Rose* by Li-Young Lee, copyright © 1986 by Li-Young Lee; "Interchanges" from *Selected Poems 1938–1988* by Yannis Ritsos, translated by Minas Savvas, edited by Kimon Friar and Kostas Myrsiades, copyright © 1989 by BOA Editions, Ltd. Reprinted by permission of BOA Editions, Ltd., www.BOAEditions.org.

Jason Bredle: "Girls, Look Out for Todd Bernstein" by Jason Bredle, originally published in *Green Mountain Review*, vol. 15, nos. 1 & 2. Reprinted by permission of the author.

Carcanet Press Limited: "The Alien" and "From Woody's Restaurant, Middlebury" from *The Ship of Birth* by Greg Delanty. Reprinted by permission of Carcanet Press Limited.

CavanKerry Press Ltd.: "Outside the Mainway Market" by Catherine Doty. Reprinted by permission of CavanKerry Press Ltd.

Tom Clark: "Nux" by Tom Clark, originally published in *Mississippi Review*, vol. 31, no. 3 (2003), copyright © 2003 by Tom Clark. Reprinted by permission of the author.

Cleveland State University Poetry Center: "What I Do" from *The Job of Being Everybody* by Douglas Goetsch, copyright © 2004 by Douglas Goetsch. Reprinted by permission of Cleveland State University Poetry Center.

Coffee House Press: "At the Cottage of Messer Violi" from *Breakers: Selected Poems* by Paul Violi, copyright © 2000 by Paul Violi. Reprinted by permission of Coffee House Press, Minneapolis, Minnesota.

Copper Beech Press: "In the Rear-View Mirror" from *Below the Surface* by Robert B. Shaw, copyright © 1999 by Robert B. Shaw. Reprinted by permission of Copper Beech Press.

Copper Canyon Press: "Heart's Itch" from *Uncertain Grace* by Rebecca Wee, copyright © 2001 by Rebecca Wee; "A Jacquard Shawl" from *Delights & Shadows* by Ted Kooser, copyright © 2003 by Ted Kooser. Reprinted by permission of Copper Canyon Press, PO Box 271, Port Townsend, Washington 98368-0271.

James Cummins: "Reading Hemingway" by James Cummins, originally published in *The Kenyon Review*—New Series, Summer, 1992, vol. XIV, no. 3. Reprinted by permission of the author.

Philip Dacey: "Thomas Eakins: A Dream of Powers" by Philip Dacey, originally published in *North American Review*, March–April 2003, copyright © 2003 by Philip Dacey. Reprinted by permission of the author.

Christina Daub: "Ibid at the Book Party" by Christina Daub, originally published in *Fulcrum*, no. 2. Reprinted by permission of the author.

Darcie Dennigan: "Eleven Thousand and One" by Darcie Dennigan. Reprinted by permission of the author.

Carl Dennis: "Amnesty" by Carl Dennis. Reprinted by permission of the author.

W. S. Di Piero: "The Little Flowers" by W. S. Di Piero, originally appeared in *Poetry* (August 2004), copyright © 2004 by W. S. Di Piero. Reprinted by permission of the author.

Gregory Djanikian: "The Soldiers" by Gregory Djanikian, originally published in *The Georgia Review*, vol. LXIII, no. 3. Reprinted by permission of the author.

Paul Durcan: "The Poetry Reading Last Night in the Royal Hibernian Hotel" from *Going Home to Russia* by Paul Durcan (The Blackstaff Press Limited, 1987), copyright © Paul Durcan. Reprinted by permission of the author.

Far Corner Books: "Famous" from *Words Under the Words: Selected Poems* by Naomi Shihab Nye, copyright © 1995. Reprinted by permission of Far Corner Books.

Farrar, Straus and Giroux, LLC: "Mrs. Darwin" from *The World's Wife* by Carol Ann Duffy, copyright © 1999 by Carol Ann Duffy; "What Is Written" from *Your Name Here* by John Ashbery, copyright © 2000 by John Ashbery; "Current" from *Streets in Their Own Ink* by Stuart Dybek, copyright © 2004 by Stuart Dybek; "Extinguishable," "Poem," and "The Fate" from *The Unsubscriber* by Bill Knott, copyright © 2004 by Bill Knott; "Instinct" and "Reading: Winter" from *Selected Poems* by C. K. Williams, copyright © 1994 by C. K. Williams; "Long Afternoons" and "Iron Train" from *Without End: New and Selected Poems* by Adam Zagajewski, translated by Clare Cavanagh, copyright © 2002 by Adam Zagajewski, translation copyright © 2002 by Farrar, Straus and Giroux, LLC. Reprinted by permission of Farrar, Straus and Giroux, LLC.

Beth Ann Fennelly: "I Need to Be More French. Or Japanese" by Beth Ann Fennelly, originally published in *Ploughshares* and *Tender Hooks* (New York: W. W. Norton, 2004). Reprinted by permission of the author.

Finishing Line Press: "Requiem" by Abigail Gramig. Reprinted by permission of Finishing Line Press, Georgetown, Kentucky.

Four Way Books: "Buddha's Dogs" from *Buddha's Dogs* by Susan Browne, copyright © 2004 by Susan Browne. All rights reserved. Reprinted by permission of the publisher.

The Gallery Press: "Retro Creation" from *Day Release* by Aidan Rooney-Céspedes. Reprinted by permission of the author and The Gallery Press, Loughcrew, Oldcastle, County Meath, Ireland.

Dan Gerber: "Why I Don't Take Naps in the Afternoon" from *A Last Bridge Home: New and Selected Poems* (Livingston, Montana: Clark City Press, 1992) by Dan Gerber, copyright © 1992 by Dan Gerber. Reprinted by permission of the author.

David R. Godine·Publisher·Incorporated: "Nothing in That Drawer" from *New & Selected Poems, 1963–1992* by Ron Padgett, copyright © 1995 by Ron Padgett. Reprinted by permission of David R. Godine, Publisher, Incorporated.

David Graham: "The Dogs in Dutch Paintings" from *Stutter Monk* by David Graham (Chico, California: Flume Press, 2000). Reprinted by permission of the author.

Graywolf Press: "At the Un-National Monument Along the Canadian Border" from *The Way It Is: New & Selected Poems* by William Stafford, copyright © 1977, 1998 by the Estate of William Stafford; "The Long Meadow" from *The Long Meadow* by Vijay Seshadri, copyright © 2004 by Vijay Seshadri; "Windowgrave" from *Still Life with Waterfall* by Eamon Grennan, copyright © 2002 by Eamon Grennan; "Happiness" from *Otherwise: New & Selected Poems* by Jane Kenyon, copyright © 1996 by the Estate of Jane Kenyon. Reprinted by permission of Graywolf Press, Saint Paul, Minnesota.

George Green: "Stephen Duck and Edward Chicken" by George Green. Reprinted by permission of the author.

Debora Greger: "Rest on the Flight into Egypt" by Debora Greger, originally published in *The Gettysburg Review* and reprinted here with the acknowledgment of the editors. Reprinted by permission of the author.

Grove/Atlantic, Inc.: "Bad Day" from *Say Uncle* by Kay Ryan, copyright © 2000 by Kay Ryan. Reprinted by permission of Grove/Atlantic, Inc.

R. S. Gwynn: "Shakespearean Sonnet" by R. S. Gwynn. Reprinted by permission of the author.

Rachel Hadas: "October Cats" by Rachel Hadas. Reprinted by permission of Rachel Hadas.

Mark Halliday: "The Current" by Mark Halliday, originally published in *Third Coast;* "Dorie Off to Atlanta" by Mark Halliday, originally published in *The Gettysburg Review.* Reprinted by permission of the author.

Hanging Loose Press: "Mishima on a Plate" by Joey Roth from *Shooting the Rat: Outstanding Poems and Stories by High School Writers*, copyright © 2003 by Hanging Loose Press. Reprinted by permission of Hanging Loose Press.

Harbour Publishing: "The Poet" from *In a Small House on the Outskirts of Heaven* by Tom Wayman, copyright © 1989 by Tom Wayman. Reprinted by permission of Harbour Publishing.

Harcourt, Inc.: "Mirrors at 4 A.M." from *The Voice at 3:00 A.M.* by Charles Simic, copyright © 2003 by Charles Simic; "Waking Late" from *Slow Air* by Robin Robertson, copyright © 2002 by Robin Robertson; "The First Photograph of Hitler" from *View With a Grain of Sand* by Wisława Szymborska, English translation by Stanislaw Baranczak and Clare Cavanagh, copyright © 1995 by Harcourt, Inc. Reprinted by permission of Harcourt, Inc.

Kerry Hardie: "Solitude" by Kerry Hardie, originally published in *Ploughshares* 30/1. Reprinted by permission of the author.

Alison Marsh Harding: "The Night of the Full Moon" by Alison Marsh Harding. Reprinted by permission of the author.

HarperCollins Publishers: "Prayer in My Boot" from *19 Varieties of Gazelle: Poems of the Middle East* by Naomi Shihab Nye, illustrated by Michael Nye, copyright © 2002 by Naomi Shihab Nye; "Snowbanks North of the House" from *Eating the Honey of Words: New and Selected Poems* by Robert Bly, copyright © 1999 by Robert Bly; "A Display of Mackerel" from *Atlantis* by Mark Doty, copyright © 1995 by Mark Doty; "Encounter" from *The Collected Poems: 1931–1987* by Czeslaw Milosz, copyright © 1988 by Czelsaw Milosz Royalties, Inc. Reprinted by permission of HarperCollins Publishers.

Bob Hicok: "To Roanoke with Johnny Cash" by Bob Hicok, originally published in *Field* #70 (Spring 2004). Reprinted by permission of the author.

Hill-Stead Museum: "Trick Pear" from *Blue Cloth* by Suzanne Cleary, copyright © 2004 by Suzanne Cleary. Reprinted by permission of Hill-Stead Museum, Farmington, CT.

The Johns Hopkins University Press: "Long Paces" and "Takeoff" from *The Color Wheel*, copyright © 1994 by Timothy Steele. Reprinted by permission of The Johns Hopkins University Press.

Houghton Mifflin Company: "To Help the Monkey Cross the River" from *The Cradle Place: Poems* by Thomas Lux, copyright © 2004 by Thomas Lux; "La Brea" from *The Boys at Twilight: Poems 1990–1995* by Glyn Maxwell, copyright © 1990, 1992, 2000 by Glyn Maxwell; "Onions" from *Search Party: Collected Poems of William Matthews* edited by Sebastian Matthews and Stanley Plumly, copyright © 2004 by Sebastian Matthews and Stanley Plumly; "Variation on the Word Sleep" from *Selected Poems II: Poems Selected and New, 1965–1975* by Margaret Atwood, copyright © 1987 by Margaret Atwood. Reprinted by permission of Houghton Mifflin Company.

Benjamin Howard: "Leaving Tralee" by Benjamin Howard, originally published in *The Recorder: The Journal of the American Irish Historical Society*, Summer 2004, copyright © 2004 by Benjamin Howard. Reprinted by permission of the author.

Christopher Howell: "Dinner Out" by Christopher Howell, originally published in *The Gettysburg Review*, vol. 17, no. 1, and reprinted here with the acknowledgment of the editors. Reprinted by permission of the author.

Bruce A. Jacobs: "Jeep Cherokee" by Bruce A. Jacobs, originally appeared in *Beloit Poetry Journal*, vol. 50, no. 4, copyright © 2000 by Bruce A. Jacobs. Reprinted by permission of the author.

Kirsten Kaschock: "Man-Made" by Kirsten Kaschock, originally published in *Gulf Coast*, vol. 17, no. 1. Reprinted by permission of the author.

David Kirby: "Mr. Dithers Explains It All to You" by David Kirby, copyright © David Kirby, and "A Cowardice of Husbands" by David Kirby, originally published in *The Georgia Review*, Summer 2003, copyright © 2003 by David Kirby. Reprinted by permission of the author.

Alfred A. Knopf, a division of Random House, Inc.: "The Clasp" from *Strike Sparks: Selected Poems, 1980–2002* by Sharon Olds, copyright © 2004 by Sharon Olds; "Unflushed Urinals" from *New and Selected Poems* by Donald Justice, copyright © 1995 by Donald Justice; "I Am Going to Start Living Like a Mystic" from *Lay Back the Darkness: Poems* by Edward Hirsch, copyright © 2003 by Edward Hirsch; "First Hour" from *The Unswept Room* by Sharon Olds, copyright © 2002 by Sharon Olds; "Boulevard du Monparnasse" from *Sunday Skaters* by Mary Jo Salter, copyright © 1994 by Mary Jo Salter; "Illumination" from *The Darkness and Light: Poems* by Anthony Hecht, copyright © 2001 by Anthony Hecht; "Muzak" from *Jelly Roll* by Kevin Young, copyright © 2003 by Kevin Young. Reprinted by permission of Alfred A. Knopf, a division of Random House, Inc.

Kenneth Koch Literary Estate: "To My Twenties" and "To Stammering" from *New Addresses* by Kenneth Koch. Reprinted by permission of the Kenneth Koch Literary Estate.

Ron Koertge: "Off-Track Betting" by Ron Koertge, originally published in *Poems & Plays*, Spring/Summer 2004. Reprinted by permission of the author.

Laurie Lamon: "Praise" by Laurie Lamon, originally published in *The Atlantic Monthly*, October 2004. Reprinted by permission of the author.

David Lehman: "Denial" by David Lehman, originally published in *Green Mountain Review*. Reprinted by permission of the author.

Margaret Levine: "In California" by Margaret Levine. Reprinted by permission of the author.

The London Review of Books: "Please Come Late" by Hugo Williams, originally published in *The London Review of Books*. Reprinted by permission of *The London Review of Books*, www.lrb.co.uk.

Louisiana State University Press: "Out There" from *The Impossible Toystore: Poems* by Mark Perlberg, copyright © 2000 by Mark Perlberg. Reprinted by permission of Louisiana State University Press.

Daniel Lusk: "Understudy" by Daniel Lusk, originally appeared in *Dakotah Territory*. Reprinted by permission of the author.

Macmillan, London, UK: "Local 32B" from *Conjure* by Michael Donaghy and "Machines" from *Dances Learned Last Night* by Michael Donaghy. Reprinted by permission of Macmillan, London, UK.

The Massachusetts Review: "the corgis of queen elizabeth" by Diane Wald, originally published in *The Massachusetts Review*, vol. 45, no. 2, Summer 2004. Reprinted by permission of *The Massachusetts Review*.

McClelland & Stewart Ltd.: "What Kind of Fool Am I?" and "A Toast to the Baltimore Oriole" from *Camber* by Don McKay. Reprinted by permission of McClelland & Stewart Ltd., *The Canadian Publishers*.

Lynne McMahon: "Wedding Ring" by Lynne McMahon, originally published in *The Gettysburg Review*, vol. 14, no. 4, and reprinted here with the acknowledgment of the editors. Reprinted by permission of the author.

Philip Memmer: "Knowledge" by Philip Memmer, originally published in *Poems & Plays*, Spring/Summer 2004. Reprinted by permission of the author.

Metre: "Arrival" by Michael Longley, originally published in *Metre #13* (Winter 02–03). Reprinted by permission of *Metre*, published at the University of Hull, England.

Robert Minhinnick: "The Fox in the National Museum of Wales" by Robert Minhinnick, originally published in *Poetry London*. Reprinted by permission of the author.

Paul Muldoon: "Soccer Moms" by Paul Muldoon, originally published in *The New Yorker*, February 16, 2004, copyright © 2004 by Paul Muldoon. Reprinted by permission of the author.

Erin Murphy: "Birthday Poem" by Erin Murphy. Reprinted by permission of the author.

Jack Myers: "Writing on Not Writing" by Jack Myers, originally published in *Poetry*, copyright © 2003 by The Modern Language Association. Reprinted by permission of the author.

W. W. Norton & Company, Inc.: "Salt Lick" from *Collected Poems 1930–1993* by May Sarton, copyright © 1993, 1988, 1984, 1980, 1974 by May Sarton; "By Daylight" from *A Woman Kneeling in the Big City* by Elizabeth Macklin, copyright © 1992 by Elizabeth Macklin; "The End and the Beginning" from *Miracle Fair* by Wisława Szymborska, translated by Joanna Trzeciak, copyright © 2001 by Joanna Trzeciak; "By Her Own Hand" from *Felt* by Alice Fulton, copyright © 2001 by Alice Fulton; "The Arm" from *Local Visitations* by Stephen Dunn, copyright © 2003 by Stephen Dunn; "Chicken" from *What Is*

This Thing Called Love: Poems by Kim Addonizio, copyright © 2004 by Kim Addonizio; "Slowly" from *Turning to Fiction: Poems* by Donna Masini, copyright © 2004 by Donna Masini; "Reading the Obituary Page" from *Last Uncle* by Linda Pastan, copyright © 2002 by Linda Pastan. Reprinted by permission of W. W. Norton & Company, Inc.

Ohio University Press: "A Monorhyme for the Shower" from *Belonging: Poems* by Dick Davis (Athens, Ohio: Swallow Press/Ohio University Press, 2002). Reprinted by permission of Swallow Press/Ohio University Press.

Ron Padgett: "Charlie Chan Wins Again" by Ron Padgett, originally published in *Court Green* (2004), copyright © 2004 by Ron Padgett. Reprinted by permission of the author.

Alan Michael Parker: "Oh, What a Red Sweater" by Alan Michael Parker. Reprinted by permission of the author.

Linda Pastan: "Leaving the Island" by Linda Pastan, originally published in *Poetry*, copyright © by Linda Pastan. Reprinted by permission of the author.

Ricardo Pau-Llosa: "Samurai" by Ricardo Pau-Llosa, originally published in *Ploughshares* 30:1, 2004, copyright © 2004 by Ricardo Pau-Llosa. Reprinted by permission of the author.

Penguin, a division of Penguin Group (USA) Inc.: "Highway 12, Just East of Paradise, Idaho," "Discretion," and "Do You Love Me?" from *Lives of the Animals* by Robert Wrigley, copyright © 2003 by Robert Wrigley; "The Invitations Overhead" from *Common Carnage* by Stephen Dobyns, copyright © 1996 by Stephen Dobyns; "He Told Her He Loved Her" from *Cemetery Nights* by Stephen Dobyns; "Why It Often Rains in the Movies" and "Request" from *Visible Signs: New and Selected Poems* by Lawrence Raab. Reprinted by permission of Penguin, a division of Penguin Group (USA) Inc.

Peter Pereira: "Anagrammer" by Peter Pereira, originally appeared in *Poetry*, September 2003, copyright © 2003 by The Poetry Foundation. Reprinted by permission of the editor of *Poetry* and the author.

Lucia Perillo: "The Floating Rib," originally published in *Shenandoah*, vol. 47, no. 1, Spring 1997, copyright © 1997 by Lucia Perillo. Reprinted by permission of Lucia Perillo.

Persea Books: "Popular Mechanics" from *Through One Tear* by Edward Nobles, copyright © 1997 by Edward Nobles. Reprinted by permission of Persea Books, Inc. (New York).

The Poetry Business: "The Foot Thing" from *Circumnavigation* by Jane Routh, copyright © Jane Routh; "The Albatross" from *The Pasta Maker* by Kate Bass, copyright © Kate Bass. Reprinted by permission of The Poetry Business.

Polygon, an imprint of Birlinn, Ltd.: "Sounds of the Day" from *Old Maps and New* by Norman MacCaig. Reprinted by permission of Polygon, an imprint of Birlinn, Ltd.

Random House, a division of Random House, Inc.: "Where Did I Leave Off?" and "Yeah, Though I Walk" from *Ants on the Melon* by Virginia Hamilton Adair, copyright © 1996 by Virginia Hamilton Adair; "Passport: A Manifesto" from *Sparrow* by Carol Muske-Dukes, copyright © 2003 by Carol Muske-Dukes. Reprinted by permission of The Random House Publishing Group, a division of Random House, Inc.

Victoria Redel: "Bedecked" from *Swoon* by Victoria Redel (Chicago, Illinois: University of Chicago Press, 2003), copyright © 2003 by Victoria Redel. Reprinted by permission of the author.

Oliver Rice: "Timely Enumerations Concerning Sri Lanka" by Oliver Rice, originally published in *The Gettysburg Review*, Summer 2004. Reprinted by permission of the author.

Pattiann Rogers: "A Traversing" from *Generations* by Pattiann Rogers (New York: Penguin, 2004), copyright © 2004 by Pattiann Rogers. Reprinted by permission of the author.

Salmon Publishing Ltd.: "The Russian Greatcoat" from *Cape Clear: New and Selected Poems* by Theodore Deppe (Ireland: Salmon Publishing, 2002). Reprinted by permission of Salmon Publishing Ltd.

Salt Publishing: "Painting a Room" and "Hurdles" from *Gogol in Rome* by Katia Kapovich (Cambridge, England: Salt Publishing, 2004). Reprinted by permission of Salt Publishing.

Sarabande Books, Inc.: "The Cove" from *The Day Before* by Dick Allen, copyright © 2003 by Dick Allen; "On Parting" from *World's Tallest Disaster* by Cate

Marvin, copyright © 2001 by Cate Marvin. "In Praise of My Young Husband" from *Bad Judgement* by Cathleen Calbert, copyright © 1999 by Cathleen Mary Calbert. Reprinted by permission of the author and Sarabande Books, Inc.

Julie Sheehan: "Hate Poem" by Julie Sheehan, originally published in *Pleiades*, vol. 24, no. 2. Reprinted by permission of the author.

Louis Simpson: "Lives of the Poets" by Louis Simpson, originally published in *Five Points*, vol. VII, no. 3. Reprinted by permission of the author.

Southern Illinois University Press: "Blurbs" from *This Country of Mothers: Poetry* by Julianna Baggott, copyright © 2001 by Julianna Baggott; "Before the Sickness Is Official" from *Misery Prefigured, Poetry* by J. Allyn Rosser, copyright © 2001 by J. Allyn Rosser. Reprinted by permission of the publisher, Southern Illinois University Press.

Gerald Stern: "Grapefruit" from *Lovesick* by Gerald Stern, copyright © 1988 by Gerald Stern. Reprinted by permission of the author.

Story Line Press: "If You Don't" from *Resistance Fantasies* by Diane Thiel; "The Busses" from *Poems for Paula* by Frederick Morgan. Reprinted by permission of Story Line Press, www.storylinepress.com.

Paul Suntup: "Olive Oil" by Paul Suntup, originally published in *Rattle*, Vol. 10, No. 1, Summer 2004, copyright © 2003 by Paul Suntup. Reprinted by permission of the author.

Joyce Sutphen: "Ever After" by Joyce Sutphen, originally published in *Poetry*, February 2003, copyright © 2003 by The Poetry Foundation. Reprinted by permission of the editor of *Poetry* and the author.

James Tate: "You Can Change Your Life Through Psychic Power" by James Tate, originally published in *The Gettysburg Review*; "The Booksigning" by James Tate, originally published in *Green Mountain Review*. Reprinted by permission of the author.

Tony Towle: "In the Coffee House" by Tony Towle, originally published in the *Mississippi Review*, vol. 31, no. 3, copyright © 2000 by Tony Towle. Reprinted by permission of the author.

Tupelo Press: "Aanabhrandhanmar Means 'Mad About Elephants'" by Aimee Nezhukumatathil, from *Miracle Fruit* (Dorset, Vermont: Tupelo Press, 2003). Reprinted by permission of Tupelo Press.

University of Akron Press: "What I Want" from *The Good Kiss* by George Bilgere, copyright © 2002 by George Bilgere; "Acceptance Speech" from *The Zones of Paradise* by Lynn Powell, copyright © 2003 by Lynn Powell. Reprinted by permission of University of Akron Press.

University of Arkansas Press: "Even Ornaments of Speech Are Forms of Deceit" from *Geography of the Forehead* by Ron Koertge, copyright © 2000 by Ron Koertge; "Tariff" from *Trembling Air* by Michelle Boisseau, copyright © 2003 by Michelle Boisseau; "Romanticism" from *Changeable Thunder* by David Baker, copyright © 2001 by David Baker. Reprinted by permission of the University of Arkansas Press.

University of California Press: "Two Disappeared into a House" from *The Selected Poetry of Yehuda Amichai, Newly Revised and Expanded Edition* by Yehuda Amichai, translated by Chana Bloch and Stephen Mitchell, copyright © 1996 by The Regents of the University of California. Reprinted by permission of the University of California Press.

University of Illinois Press: "Late Valentine, with Daisies" from *Chance Ransom: Poems* by Kevin Stein, copyright © 2000 by Kevin Stein. Reprinted by permission of the poet and the University of Illinois Press.

University of Pittsburgh Press: "What I Did" from *Blessing the House* by Jim Daniels, copyright © 1997. Reprinted by permission of the University of Pittsburgh Press.

University of Washington Press: "Keats" from *Light's Ladder* by Christopher Howell, copyright © by Christopher Howell. Reprinted by permission of the University of Washington Press.

Verse Press: "Bohemian Blues" from *Monkey Time* by Philip Nikolayev, copyright © 2003 by Philip Nikolayev. Reprinted by permission of the author and Verse Press.

Paul Violi: "Appeal to the Grammarians" by Paul Violi, originally published in *Green Mountain Review*, copyright © Paul Violi. Reprinted by permission of the author.

Wesleyan University Press: "National Cold Storage Company" from *National Cold Storage Company* by Harvey Shapiro, copyright © 1988 by Harvey Shapiro; "Passenger Pigeons" from *At the Edge of Orchard Country* by Robert Morgan. Reprinted by permission of Wesleyan University Press.

Franz Wright: "Publication Date" by Franz Wright, originally published in *Field* magazine. Reprinted by permission of Franz Wright.

The Wylie Agency, Inc.: "To the Dust of the Road" by W. S. Merwin, originally published in *Poetry,* vol. CLXXXII, no. 6, September 2003, copyright © 2003 by W. S. Merwin. Reprinted by permission of The Wylie Agency, Inc.

Dean Young: "I Said Yes But I Meant No" by Dean Young. Reprinted by permission of the author.

Zoo Press: "Air Larry" from *Someone Else's Name* by Joseph Harrison, copyright © 2004 by Joseph Harrison. All rights reserved. Reprinted by permission of Zoo Press.